"Forget boring self-help books! *Three Seconds of Courage* is a captivating adventure that shows how anyone can be brave. Riley Kehoe's story is like a movie you can't stop watching, filled with relatable struggles and heart-pounding moments. By the end, you'll be cheering yourself on, ready to tackle your own fears. This book is a must-read for anyone who wants to live a bolder, braver life!"

Bob Goff, *New York Times* bestselling author of *Love Does*,
Everybody Always, *Dream Big*, and *Undistracted*

"Riley Kehoe is a woman who is marked by courage and a woman who gives courage to others, through the hope and joy of Jesus Christ. In her book *Three Seconds of Courage*, Riley shares her own journey of overcoming fear and stepping into courage, even in the midst of chaos and catastrophe. Her story is unlike anything you've heard and will leave you inspired, encouraged, and expectant."

Madison Prewett Troutt, author, speaker,
podcast host, and TV personality

"In an age where fear is pervasive, we all need more reminders to be brave. Riley's insightful wisdom, hard-won through unspeakable circumstances, illuminates how small, purposeful acts of courage can profoundly transform your life. Her words are not only vulnerable and raw, they are a rallying call for anyone who wants to build a more resilient spirit through the power of showing up—a few intentional seconds at a time."

Hannah Brencher, author of *The Unplugged Hours*

"This book is for anyone ready to challenge themselves, learn more about themselves, and say YES to courage and NO to fear. I have seen Riley live out these tips and stories and change people's lives with her boldness and courage in the process, and now she's going to do the same for you with this book!"

Jeanine Amapola Ward, author, speaker,
podcaster, and Christian influencer

"I couldn't put Riley's story of courage down. This book is a treasure that I pray will reach many hearts and minds to live boldly for Jesus! Riley makes you feel included and never forgotten. Her words are sweet to the soul and full of life!

I have had the joy of witnessing Riley's love in action and bravery up close. Her bravery made me want to be brave too! I couldn't be more grateful for her YES to Jesus. God's miracle-working power shines through her life! God is with you and for you. Take a leap of faith! On the other side of your courageous heart is a wonderful adventure! 3, 2, 1 . . . Jump!"

Meredith Foster, YouTuber, podcast host, and social media influencer

"This book can absolutely change your life! Everyone wants to be fearless and live purposefully. Unfortunately, few actually unlock that treasure. Riley Kehoe is one of the few. She has a gift for using her life story to guide us into the contagious courage we all long for. I can't wait to see how this book transforms your life."

Daniel Fusco, pastor, author, and TV and radio host

"Riley's book is a must for anyone who is seeking truth, boldness, and bravery. She is a gifted storyteller and adventurer, and this book is a must-read for everyone but especially for young women seeking to grow in their walk with Christ. Riley feels like a trusted friend and big sister through her storytelling and ability to write with a gentle, strong, adventurous, and engaging tone."

Grace Valentine, author, blogger, podcast host, and speaker

"An invitation requires a response and who invites you matters. This book is an invitation to overcome fear, walk with courage, and live a life fully alive. Riley not only extends this invitation to you from her own journey but also from a place of actively living out what she writes. I can't recommend this book enough to souls longing for more than the average mundane and status quo."

Zack Curry, lead pastor, Jesus Culture San Diego

"Riley is fully alive and fully courageous, and she injects the world with life wherever she goes. Riley's story gives her the power and authority to teach us how to live with full courage as well. Read these words and let her shock you back to life!"

Daniel Grothe, associate senior pastor,
New Life Church, Colorado Springs, CO

"In *Three Seconds of Courage*, Riley Kehoe takes us on a riveting journey through the highs and lows of facing fear head-on. Her authentic and heartfelt storytelling will inspire readers to embrace their own moments of courage. This book is a testament to the human spirit and the incredible things we can achieve when we take that leap of faith."

Kait Tomlin, bestselling author, dating coach,
and founder of Heart of Dating

"Concerning times require courage. Not brash strength but gentle, confident intentionality. Riley has such a counselor spirit as she vulnerably shares her story and elicits a timely assessment of our heart and motive in today's world. I'm thankful for her encouraging wisdom as a young leader."

Grant Skeldon, Next Gen Director at THINQ
and author of *The Passion Generation*

"Challenged and changed. Those are the two words that come to mind when I think how Riley has impacted me. Not only have I personally experienced the 'Call Up' that comes along with doing life with Riley but I have also witnessed how Riley's presence alone challenges and changes everyone around her. If you are looking to strengthen your faith, become bolder and more courageous in your daily life, and truly walk in wisdom with bold confidence, then this book is for you! I know from personal experience that you will be both challenged and changed because of it."

Tori Masters, Christian influencer and YouTuber

"In a generation and culture where fear seems to be the prevailing narrative, we must never forget the truth—that courage is at the core of every person who desires to live a life of purpose and destiny. Fear is your past, and courage is your future."

Ross Johnston, revivalist and cofounder of CA Will Be Saved

"Prepare to delve into layers of emotion, hope, and self-discovery. Riley Kehoe's *Three Seconds of Courage* will take you on a journey few have witnessed. Discover courage within yourself and build resilience through the power of prayer and connection."

Kevin Briggs, Sergeant, California Highway Patrol (Ret.)
and author of *Guardian of the Golden Gate*

Three
Seconds
of
Courage

How Small Acts of Bravery
Lead to Big Change

RILEY KEHOE
WITH NATALIE HANEMANN

BakerBooks

a division of Baker Publishing Group
Grand Rapids, Michigan

Published by Baker Books
a division of Baker Publishing Group
Grand Rapids, Michigan
BakerBooks.com

Library of Congress Cataloging-in-Publication Data
Names: Kehoe, Riley, 1994– author.
Title: Three seconds of courage : how small acts of bravery lead to big change / Riley Kehoe.
Description: Grand Rapids, Michigan : Baker Books, a division of Baker Publishing Group, [2025] | Includes bibliographical references.
Identifiers: LCCN 2024022193 | ISBN 9781540904270 (paper) | ISBN 9781540904737 (casebound) | ISBN 9781493449101 (ebook)
Subjects: LCSH: Kehoe, Riley, 1994– | Christian biography—United States. | Courage—Religious aspects—Christianity.
Classification: LCC BR1725.K44 A3 2025 | DDC 270.092 [B]—dc23/eng/20240628
LC record available at https://lccn.loc.gov/2024022193

Published in association with The Bindery Agency, www.TheBinderyAgency.com.

25   26   27   28   29   30   31   7   6   5   4   3   2   1

CONTENTS

INTRODUCTION

"You are worth a life filled with joy and peace."

The other day, my best friend asked me, "What would your sixteen-year-old self find most surprising about your life today?"

I laughed and said, "Pretty much everything, but mostly that I'm not scared anymore."

I used to be scared of a lot of things: death, rejection, the ocean, not being good enough, being bullied. I was so afraid of sadness that I actively pretended to be happy, and I was even afraid of balloons (more on that to come!). Sometimes, I still feel like that terrified sixteen-year-old girl with braces who was socially awkward and couldn't pronounce words correctly.

If you're scared too, well, welcome to the club. If you're in a space that's lonely and frightening, I know how you feel. This world can be savage. I've been in the trenches of fear. I know what it looks like. I stayed there for years. But I crawled out, and you can too. It won't happen in a day. If you are anything like me, it will take you months or years. But it's worth the effort because on the other side of your fear is freedom.

You are worth a life filled with joy and peace. You are worth living a life you're proud of. You are worth the investment of reading all the words in this book.

Words have the power to change our lives. I was in a position of paralyzing fear when my dad said a few words that changed the trajectory of my life: "Riley, either courage or fear will exist in your life, and you get to choose which one wins. All you need is a little more courage."

Since then, I think of fear and courage as being in an ongoing battle, and victory comes by reaching down deeper to eke out just a little more courage. This truth is the North Star I follow, and doing so has given me extraordinary experiences, which you'll read about in the pages ahead.

Imagine what your life would look like if you had a little more courage to

chase after the job you want,
walk away from the friends who aren't good for you,
not let a good opportunity pass by,
share your hidden talent with the world,
jump at a new job in a new city,
or, perhaps, to simply say no.

The difference between the life you want and the life you're currently living hinges on your finding courage: one small act that has a big impact.

I spent years asking myself why I should bother fighting this battle over fear. You and I both know it's far easier to let fear consume us. But deep down, we also know we were made for more. Something within us wants to resist giving in to our fears. We want to leap. We want to argue. We aren't happy living in the mundane. We are compelled to fight back.

Our lives aren't the only ones at risk of being mundane. The world waits, desperately relying on us to win the battle between playing it safe and going all in with living boldly. One ordinary person with courage can alter the future of an entire community.

I feel I should warn you: some of the stories you're about to read will be disturbing. I can make you a promise, though. I will always be honest with you. I will not sugarcoat my life's most challenging moments. I only hope my honesty will allow you to be truthful about your own story. This is me showing you my heart. This is not a book filled with small talk. At times it's deep, raw, and intense. But at other times, especially the embarrassing moments, I hope you will laugh with me.

One of my writing mentors told me to tell a story of where I failed in the first few chapters. I laugh now, because I don't tell you only one story, but many. It was easy to think of a failure moment; I've had countless. So, my friend, let me tell you about some of the potholes I fell into in the hope that you can jump over a few of your own.

One other warning: this book is me reflecting on my life from an adult perspective, but because I was a child when I experienced some of these events, some minor details may not be entirely accurate. I try my best to always be truthful, but if I get some things wrong, it's because my childlike mind didn't process the events with exactness.

Oh, and if I could go back in time, there's one more thing I'd tell my sixteen-year-old self: "Riley, when you figure out how to abandon your fear and let courage be your beacon, your life will become one big, wild, wonderful adventure. It's there waiting for you. You just have to believe it for it to be true."

Courage has an adventure waiting for you too. 3-2-1!

1

Christmas in Thailand

"Don't worry, it's an earthquake. It's okay, we're fine."

shouldn't be alive today. And there is quite a story to tell between my love of the ocean and my fear and reckoning with the time it nearly took my life—and did take the lives of countless others.

I will tell this story soon, but it begins with my core love of surfing.

Somebody once asked me where I feel the most like myself, and without hesitating, I responded, "In the ocean, on a surfboard."

Surfing has for many years been like my inhale in life; it is the one thing that fills and lifts my heart and body, making me buoyant. When I'm in the ocean—the warmth of the sun hitting my shoulders, the salt water beading on my skin, my legs submerged, and my eyes watching, waiting for that wave—I am present in a way that makes time fall away and distractions disappear. I can focus only on the right now.

I don't bring a single worry into the ocean; I leave those on the sand. The instant my feet get wet, I am free. Surfing is my safe place, which is ironic given the story I'm about to share. I am drawn to the water itself, the vastness of the ocean. I respect the ocean and how unpredictable it is. But that unpredictability is why I can go in every single day and never have the same experience. I never know what to expect. I'm sure this level of confidence comes from growing up having never lived farther than an hour from its shore.

However, I haven't always felt safe in the ocean. There was a time when I knew it to be a place of danger, a source of destruction and death. This is the lesson the ocean taught me when I was ten years old.

~~~

When I was young, my family often traveled to Thailand around Christmastime to visit my grandfather. He lived there for half the year, and the other half he spent in Italy. He told us he was "following the sun."

My grandfather had worked in the Office of Naval Intelligence in the US Navy, but as a kid, I was convinced he was an American CIA agent. He was an unforgettable person who was always on the go. But so are all of my family members. My mum is a fierce powerhouse who loves people without limits. In life, she takes the bull by the horns and fights back. My dad is the quiet one, but when he speaks, wisdom and brilliance flow. I have two younger sisters. Sierra, the middle sibling, is thoughtful, intelligent, and deeply empathetic. I've always been in awe of her memory. To prepare for an exam in school, she'd just read over her notes and let her photographic memory kick in. I am pretty sure Sierra will cure cancer one day. My youngest sister, Bronte, is fun and the most determined person you'll ever meet. It doesn't matter what she does; once she puts her mind to it, it's game over.

My parents highly emphasized service, and we often went on family volunteer trips throughout the year. In 2004 when we visited my grandfather, we spent part of our time working in an orphanage called Zoe House with kids who had been rescued from human trafficking.

At the orphanage, I met a girl my age named Dara. We had so much in common. We loved playing outside on the swings, and we would do that for hours. But there was one thing we didn't have in common. She was pregnant. I was too young to fully understand how she came to be in that situation or the trauma she must have experienced. But I was happy to have met her and to have a friend to play with on those days we volunteered.

We stayed at the orphanage for a week, making meals, doing dishes, cleaning toilets, and playing with the kids. My mum encouraged the volunteers and leaders and shared with them her years of experience in kids' ministry. My sisters and I prayed for the kids while my dad quietly cared for the many practical needs of the orphanage and ministered to the people through one-on-one conversation. Following our time at Zoe House, we had booked a Christmas family holiday with my grandfather and my mum's extended side of the family.

A couple of days before Christmas Eve, we traveled from the orphanage in a tuktuk, which is a little car that looks like an extended golf cart. Our driver swerved around other vehicles, honking and gesturing, giving what seemed like an animated performance for his tourist passengers. All the other drivers behaved the same—driving in Thailand is chaotic. Eventually, the tuktuk dropped us at the shoreline where we walked into the water, climbed into a boat, and headed for Railay Beach.

As we skirted around several of the small islands that pepper the Thailand shore, I sat perched at the front of the boat while my dad affectionately rubbed my back, marveling at the crystal-clear water and watching the fish swimming alongside the boat. There are literally hundreds of islands off the mainland, some too small to step on and some big enough to hold multiple resorts. I took in my surroundings, admiring the high limestone cliffs that surrounded each island, the thick trees with leaves every shade of green, and the caves carved into the sides of the cliffs where I imagined mermaids lived. I heard the monkeys in the trees and saw seabirds gliding from one island to the next.

When we finally arrived, my mum's side of the family was eagerly awaiting us. I jumped out of the boat and ran to my grandfather, who gave me a huge bear hug. I felt light-hearted because while we'd worked at the orphanage, a level of heaviness was ever-present, even when I was playing with the kids. When Grandpa hugged me, though, it seemed all my burdens disappeared. There I was, with my beloved family on this beautiful beach.

Railay Beach, where the resort is situated, is on a peninsula, but it feels like an island because the only way to reach it is by boat. The jungle is so dense that roads to the next closest town have not been built. The area by the bay is flat with two cliffs flanking the resorts, so it felt like we were between two mountains. Once we were all off the boat, we grabbed our suitcases and headed to the check-in desk for our beachfront bungalows. When my mum let the receptionist know we had arrived, I could tell from the expression on the woman's face that something was wrong. After speaking with someone next to her in rushed Siamese, she turned to my mum and haltingly explained that they were very sorry, but they'd accidentally double-booked us.

My grandfather had made this reservation the year before, but they'd already given the bungalow intended for our family to another party. They offered to put us up in a room offering ocean views on the top floor of a concrete apartment building in the middle of the resort. My parents didn't get frustrated or make a scene. My mum thanked them and took the keys.

～

On Christmas Day, the family gathered at one of my aunties' bungalows near the beach. I was given wonderful presents, but the one I remember most clearly was a set of red candy-cane pajamas. The day passed with me eating copious amounts of chocolate and opening gifts. There were twelve of us, and I loved being around so many relatives. The weather was beautiful and sunny, so we went swimming and snorkeling. At the end of the day, I put on my new pj's and drifted to sleep, listening as the adults relaxed and enjoyed the start of a family holiday. My dad later carried me back to our apartment. Through my sleepiness, I recall him tucking me into bed and kissing my forehead.

Right before dawn, I woke up to sudden shaking. I immediately assumed my little sister Bronte was underneath my bed playing a joke on me. I jumped off and squatted to catch her in the act, but she wasn't there. Suddenly the ground began to rumble, and I became very confused. My thoughts were spinning as I tried to make sense of what was happening. Some of the decorations on the wall started crashing to the floor. I managed to run down the hallway into my parents' room, and the moment I opened the door, the shaking stopped. My mum was sitting up in bed, and she looked at me with a tender expression and said, "Don't worry, it's an earthquake. It's okay, we're fine."

My dad came over to hug me and tell me we were safe. My two younger sisters, who had also been startled awake, trailed behind me. We listened as Mum called reception and asked for details on the episode. The hotel confirmed that there had been an earthquake. My mum asked, "Have you heard if there are any more coming?" The resort employees reassured her that everything was fine, and it had been just an unexpected one-off. "Carry on with your day," the receptionist assured her, so I ran off to put on my swimsuit.

A short while later, we all left for breakfast. I was thrilled to see that it included a chocolate fountain, and I forgot about the earthquake. I filled my plate with chocolate-dipped strawberries and waffles and French toast. I put way more food on my plate than my little ten-year-old stomach could handle. After all that sugar, we embarked on a boat trip to explore Koh Khai, also known as Egg Island—a tiny isle of sand in the middle of the ocean. Back at Railay Beach later on, my parents relaxed on the shore, engrossed in their books, while my sisters and I played in the sand.

A little while later, my parents walked to the beachfront reception area to borrow the front desk phone and call the airlines to confirm the return flights we'd be taking in a couple of days. While my mum was on hold, my dad asked her about the plan for the day. She responded, "We have rock climbing booked for you and me in a few hours. The girls are all on the beach making sandcastles. If they're content, just let them keep playing." That was standard for my parents—they encouraged us to play and didn't often disrupt us if things were going smoothly. My dad came to find us and saw we were happily playing, but for some reason, he felt prompted to tell us, "Girls, it's time to go to the room," and so we hopped up and followed him, no questions asked.

Railay Beach, located near Phuket Island, is so small and flat that from our apartment in the middle of the resort, through the palm trees, we could just see the beaches on both sides. As my dad, sisters, and I started walking back to the room, I noticed something odd. I couldn't hear any animal sounds. The area had a ton of monkeys, and normally they were quite noisy. Now, it was strangely silent. I noticed a dog that was standing still. He howled as if he'd been hurt, and then whimpered. An instant later, he ran into the forest. The birds that had been chirping earlier were now flying off. It created an eerie feeling. Something was in the air. I noticed all this but didn't say anything and kept following Dad.

In the haunting silence, we started hearing people scream and shout. We knew immediately something was very wrong. I looked over my shoulder toward the beach—and where the water had just been there was now only sand. All the water around the beach had left. My mind couldn't make sense of what my eyes were seeing. Fish were flopping around on the wet sand. Boats were now sitting on the shore. Snorkelers were stuck out on reefs. I watched while people started to run in all directions; nobody seemed to know what was going on.

When I took a closer look at where the sand ended, I saw a thin white line in the distance and, somehow, the white line was growing bigger and bigger by the second. I looked up at

THREE SECONDS OF COURAGE

my dad and asked him where Mum was. He began looking around, and I started shouting for her as loud as I could.

My mother told us later that she'd hung up on the airline when the water started to recede and knew instantly what was happening. She remembered seeing a sign on a beach in Florida that explained when the water leaves, you have only a few minutes to get to high ground.

She ran to where she thought my sisters and I were building sandcastles. Hundreds of people were panicking around her, shouting and shoving and falling down. When she got to the exact spot she'd last seen us, we weren't there. She started to freak out but stopped herself. In the middle of the chaos, she asked the Lord, "Where are they?" and she heard one word: *flee*. Now she was faced with the decision to either run to safety or keep trying to find me and my sisters. But she trusted the word in her head, sprinting back in the direction of the apartment.

The white line I'd seen was a giant tsunami plowing directly at our resort. We frantically looked for my mum, and I suddenly spotted her rushing from the beach toward us. Her urgent shouts of "Run!" pierced through the chaos as she desperately tried to alert everyone of the impending danger. I will never forget the look on her face. Her eyes were wide with fear.

I had never seen my mum rattled, so to see her like that took my fear to another level. When she reached us at the entrance to our apartment, she grabbed my sister's hand and sprinted down the path. Before we started running, I noticed my dad do the strangest thing. He turned around and locked the door to the apartment. I couldn't understand it because it seemed so unimportant when we were supposed to have been running for our lives! Later on, we learned what a wise decision he'd made; after a natural disaster, there's often looting.

The five of us took off toward the other side of the resort, which didn't take long because the peninsula is very narrow. My mum ran holding my sister Bronte and my dad held Sierra. I ran between them. As the wave struck the beach behind us, I heard the sounds of wood being crushed from crumpling buildings and the screams from those who had not acted quickly enough. Already we could see people being struck by the wave and the debris. It was awful and scary, and I know now they probably did not survive.

As we stood on the beach on the other side of the peninsula, we saw that the fast-moving wave was still barreling toward us like a massive wall. It's hard to explain just how powerful that much water can be, but World Vision later wrote, "The Sumatra-Andaman earthquake, which caused the 2004 Indian Ocean tsunami, is estimated to have released energy equivalent to 23,000 Hiroshima-type atomic bombs."[1] The first time I read that, I cried.

We paused for a moment to figure out our location. The wave was now about three hundred meters (around one thousand feet or three football fields) from where we stood—the water full of debris and bodies from the path it had consumed. Then I noticed a man in a boat sitting on the sand. He got out of the boat, maybe thinking he could make it to higher ground in time. But then he stopped, turned, and started to return to his boat. Maybe he thought he could hide in it. I will never forget the feeling I had as we watched the wave hit his boat, which instantly exploded into a thousand pieces. He was violently thrown into the pounding wave. His body, the blood, and the pieces of wood and metal from the boat all scattered as the wave charged forward. At that moment, I realized the imminence of the danger we were still facing—my life and the lives of my entire family were on the line.

I can't tell this story without sharing some of the coincidences that occurred. I believe coincidences are small miracles in which God chooses to remain hidden. An hour before the tsunami struck, our family had returned from exploring Egg Island, where we most certainly would not have survived if we had still been there when the wave hit. The day before, on Christmas Day, my mum and I had gone for a hike and gotten lost on one of the hills on the peninsula. We found this goat path, a beaten-down trail where hikers must have cleared a narrow walkway. It led up one of the cliffs on the southern side of the peninsula by the sea. With the wave gaining on us, my mum looked at me and shouted, "Riley, the goat path! We need to find it." I remembered where it was and started running, the roaring sound of the crashing water chasing us, echoing off the cliffs on both sides.

It was common to see life jackets hanging on poles around the resort, and my mum saw one and grabbed it, slipping it over my head. A moment later, a Thai woman ran up to me and tried to get the life jacket off me. I gripped it hard and we tugged back and forth. I remember she looked at me with eyes as big as coconuts and ripped that life jacket off me and ran.

Even with my parents carrying the extra weight of my sisters, I was falling behind. My body was tired, but my instincts told me I could not let myself slow down. We kept running through the forest looking for that goat path, and I remember praying the whole time, *Lord, help us find this pathway.* By the grace of God, we did come upon it and started climbing.

Years later, my little sister Bronte, who was five when all this happened, was asked what she remembers from that day. She told people over and over again the one thing she remembered most clearly was my prayers as we ran up that goat path. While we sprinted and grabbed onto tree limbs and pulled ourselves up as fast as we could, she said I just kept shouting, "God, help us! Lord, rescue us. We need You!"

As we trekked up the cliffside, my dad was holding my seven-year-old sister Sierra. I'm still not sure how she managed it, but as she was holding on to my dad, she was also holding a small kid's bucket full of water. In the bucket, in the midst of this chaos, my sister had managed to rescue some of the fish that were landlocked from the water rapidly receding. Carrying this bucket was slowing us down, and my dad told her to let it go, but Sierra furrowed her brow and frowned. She grasped the bucket tighter and shouted, "The fishes will survive." As my dad ran, the bucket jiggled so violently that the fish flopped to and fro, and my sister shifted the bucket back and forth to keep them safely inside. While chaos and terror reigned around us, my sweet little sister had poured all her empathy, focus, and willpower into saving those fish. In an incredible act of understanding, my dad did not force her to let go of them.

The tsunami was so powerful that it caused the entire ground to shake. As we climbed higher up the path, we prayed we'd be high enough above the spot where the wave crested.

There was one moment when I looked back down to the beach, and I instantly wished I hadn't. Our altitude afforded a grand view of the resort, and what I saw was like a scene from the apocalypse. The wave was annihilating everything in its way—people, animals, buildings, boats.

My dad noticed that I was falling behind; I had no energy left. As a ten-year-old, I was nowhere near as strong as either of my parents, even with them carrying my sisters. And then I heard my dad's voice, deep and commanding: "Riley! Run!"

And just like that, I focused on my father's voice and let the chaos around me fall away. I zoned in on his words and his location, five steps ahead of me. I sped up to catch up to him. The massive swell of white water was at my back. I ran and ran and ran—and by the grace of God, we got high enough that the wave couldn't reach us. We were just over a hundred feet from ground level.

I got my second wind and kept running, passing both my parents before reaching the top of the hill—far, far above the water below—where the forest ended and opened up to a grassy area. The sun was shining across a clear blue sky. Surrounding the grassy patch were trees that blocked most views of the surrounding beaches.

The first thing I did when my feet hit the grass was fall to my knees. I folded my hands and bowed my head. I had just been rescued. That prayer was the closest I've ever come in my life to experiencing the Lord tangibly. I prayed for God to continue to help us; I thanked Him for saving us and asked for His peace. My heart cried out to Him. Then I felt what I can only describe as a blanket being wrapped around me. It was His wraparound, loving presence.

The whole area was still rumbling from the force of the tsunami, and yet I was unshakable. I felt such peace. I went from being covered in sweat, heart racing, brain in a fog from shock, feeling like I was about to die, to this moment of prayer where my heart, mind, and body settled. There was no way I could understand what we'd just lived through, but I had a gut feeling that while I couldn't comprehend it, everything was going to be okay, no matter the outcome.

My mum and dad and sisters caught up and ran to where I was praying, and we threw our arms around one another. I could see just how much danger we'd escaped from my parents' expressions.

My mum leaned over and kissed my forehead—a tender act in the midst of utter devastation. We had made it. But my heart kept remembering the scenes I wish I could forget— because so many others hadn't made it. Now, cradling the weight of survival, I wonder, *Was I saved for a reason?* My prayer now is that I may find the strength to live a life worthy of the miracle I've been given.

2

A Courageous Life
Is a Wild Adventure

*"A little bit of courage in your daily choices goes
a long way, like baking soda in a cake."*

When I was seven, my family moved to a large farm in Auckland, and we kids loved it. "We'll be back later, Mum!" I shouted as my two younger sisters and I ran out the door into the New Zealand sunshine wearing our gum boots (long rubber boots) because it rained at some point nearly every day.

"What's the one thing you need to remember?" Mum yelled back.

"If in doubt, pray."

My sisters and I didn't have cell phones back then, but a huge level of confidence in Jesus made this kind of freedom possible. We lived in the middle of nowhere or, as we like to call it in New Zealand, the wop-wops. There was no reception on the farm.

Living on a farm created endless hours of fun for me and my sisters and boundless ways to test our courage. We thrived in a playful haven my parents built, where we were always free to be kids. We had very few rules around the farm. Once we got outside, we were free to explore for hours. My parents trusted us despite the amount of trouble three young kids could get into. We played with bows and arrows, crossbows, knives, and machetes; we rode horses bareback without helmets; we trampled through poisonous plant life. We were explorers, wild and free. Boredom breeds curiosity, and curiosity activates the imagination.

My sisters and I would make our way into the outlying fields that made up twenty acres of our property, patting my beloved horse, Charlie, on the head as we passed by while our sweet boxer, Rosie, who was graying around the eyes, trailed slowly behind us. The farm was home to cattle, horses, chickens, sheep, and goats. Beyond the stables and fenced-in fields was the mysterious forest that went on so far it felt like we would never reach the end of it.

To get to the forest, we had to cross a river by balancing and walking across fallen trees. We loved to fill our time playing a game we called Survivors. We would create whole new personas and go live off the land—with the aid of some packed snacks and water bottles. Sometimes we did this for a few hours, and sometimes we'd be gone all day. We imagined no other humans were alive on earth.

We often got lost in the forest, but somehow after hours of trudging along and trying to track our footprints, we'd find our way home—mostly because Rosie would guide us back to base. It was worth the risk to exercise our independence and let our imaginations run wild. Injuries never deterred us from getting right back to our adventure.

Our "base" was a tree house our dad had built—an open platform situated between limbs of a broad oak tree that was reached by climbing a ladder. The tree house was just past the river, near where we'd buried our beloved pigs, Sausage and Ham. (Don't worry, they'd lived happy lives and died fat and of natural causes.)

Up in the tree house, we imagined being overrun by zombies, and we'd let Rosie attack the undead with her magically powered bark that had the ability to scare zombies away. We used branches for swords and played The Floor is Lava, swinging vine to vine through the kauri trees like Tarzan.

When playing, we referred to one another only by our persona names, which happened to also be our middle names. Our personas had entirely different personalities from our natural-born traits. Mine was named Elizabeth, and she was the epitome of courage in my young mind and everything I wanted to be. I am partially deaf (though it wouldn't be diagnosed for a couple years), and that made me awkward socially. I was a bit insecure about my body. It probably didn't help that my mum styled my hair in pigtails or that I wore a massive backpack with four hip and body straps or that I carried my Bible wherever I went. In truth, Riley was someone I was a little ashamed of. Elizabeth, though, was courageous, assertive, and strong.

At first, acting like Elizabeth was a role reserved for when we played Survivor, but eventually, the acting gave way. At school when I felt shy or awkward, I would ask myself, *What would Elizabeth do in this situation?* Or when I got bullied, I'd wonder, *How would Elizabeth respond?* Something about the repetitive nature of knowingly pretending helped me to eventually become the main character in my life story.

One reason I was eventually able to become more like Elizabeth is because my family moved around quite a bit. I regularly found myself in the role of "the new girl" and needed to put myself out there and make new friends. It seemed my parents would long for a new adventure after living in a place for too long. But the impact of moving so often wasn't always positive. It affected me and my sisters, each in varying ways based on our personalities. Always having boxes that hadn't been unpacked remained an indicator of a life not fully settled.

As a kid, "home" was sometimes fluid. Not my homelife or family dynamics, but literally, home could be as big as a house or as small as a piece of luggage. And it changed often between the two. It's natural to think about home in the sense of a physical location. It's also natural to wonder if home is a place of safety and security. If home is constantly moving and changing, then sometimes it doesn't feel so safe.

When my mum found out she was pregnant with me, my parents moved from Hong Kong to London, believing England to be an idyllic location to raise a child. I spent the first five years of my life in a funky little house called Tumbleweed Cottage in a country village outside of London. Across the street was a park with a forest, and black-faced sheep moved freely around the neighborhood. It was everything one would imagine a classic English village to be. While there, Sierra and Bronte also arrived into the world. I was so excited to have two new playmates and automatic best friends!

When I was five, we left England and moved to a cozy home on a lake in the mountains of Los Angeles County. My mum is a major health freak, being stubbornly organic even before it was in vogue—from her diet and fashion choices to her lack of makeup and refusal to have any cosmetic work done. The natural beauty of that area—the mountains, the water—made our hippie community seem the perfect place for her three daughters to enjoy childhood. Evidently, the other mums in the area weren't so interested in my mum's motto to "grow old gracefully." My parents hoped to raise my sisters and me in a humble, down-to-earth community, but they didn't find it there. After two years in Los Angeles, we left America for New Zealand.

Soon after we arrived in New Zealand, my parents enrolled us in a small rural school. Imagine the extreme of going from an LA elementary school where some students were dropped off by a driver to a rural farm school where kids showed up shoeless and on horses. My first farm school project was to raise a calf—I'm guessing I would have never gotten that assignment in Los Angeles.

In New Zealand, my parents enjoyed flipping homes, so we didn't stay in one place longer than three years. We also traveled a lot; volunteering and vacations took us to many places. Several times we spent our entire summer in a different country.

As children, we asked our parents why we traveled so much, and my dad said that travel was part of our education and that we became better people based on our experiences. Looking back now, I have to agree. I loved seeing different places and learning about new cultures. I got to meet new people, try new foods, and see some of the most beautiful places on the planet.

Throughout all our travels, I worked hard to become more like my Elizabeth persona: strong, valiant, and gutsy. Eventually, I succeeded. But now she has a new name. Now, it is

Riley. But I'll let you in on a little secret. Even to this day, while that awkward, quiet Riley may be gone, I still battle between two personas—my true self and the shy, more fearful version that it is sometimes easier to be.

These formative years provided a solid foundation for me to practice what would become my heart's battle cry: courage. Moving to various countries shaped in me a view that life is one big adventure, and luckily, courage isn't boring. Limiting the amount of material items we owned helped us stay nimble. It takes courage to be adaptable.

My family hoped to leave seeds of love in the heart of each person we met. Imagine the wind blowing over a dandelion puff, scattering the little seeds along on the breeze to new locations. They go where the wind takes them. Now imagine an oak tree, huge, majestic, and only ever staying in one place. Being a tree isn't bad, but there may come a time when God wants you to be the dandelion and go someplace new, leaving the seeds of your love at a fresh destination. Have you ever desired to move to a different city or country? Perhaps there are hearts in another place waiting for your seeds of love.

It's easy to live on autopilot, but it comes with the danger of life getting monotonous. Courage pushes us into an unpredictable life. I spell courage as R-I-S-K. Friend, don't let life drift by you. In truth, we aren't just along for the ride. We're sitting in the driver's seat. And living a life of adventure means we have to leave the parking lot.

My parents taught me that one of the wildest and most rewarding adventures in life is love and marriage. Something my parents did every week was have a date night. My sisters and I loved that because we had a babysitter who'd let us stay up late watching movies and eating sweets. Mum and Dad would get all dressed up and tell us to have fun. The way they looked at each other . . . it was pure adoration. They made it clear that their marriage was more important than anything else, and we weren't offended by not being their number one priority. They explained that if their marriage was good, and if they loved one another and kept their connection strong, they'd be better parents. And then we, as the by-product, would feel more loved. At the time, I didn't realize how much of a gift a loving marriage is for a child. They showed me that no marriage haphazardly drifts toward holiness and harmony; it takes work. As a young adult, their love was the hope and standard in dating that safeguarded me from potential heartbreak.

On the farm in New Zealand, I was so excited to come home after school. I watched my dad kiss my mum at the front door before he embraced us kids in a hug. Then I ripped off my school uniform, threw on old clothes and gum boots, and rushed outside to be with the animals. My fat pony, Charlie, was an Appaloosa covered in brown and black spots, and he was my best friend and safe place. In the muddy fields with a thick scent of horse manure, I found my peace. Surrounded by pigs, chickens, horses, and sheep, I felt the freedom to be my true self and express my emotions. Animals don't judge! After the tsunami, the farm would be my refuge to heal.

The favorite pastime of me and one of my sisters was to play with Peter, our ram. It is no exaggeration to say Peter had anger issues. He would ram anybody who stepped into his paddock. Peter had no chill; he was always aggressive. We invented this game where we put on helmets, got into his paddock, got on our hands and knees a few feet away, and charged him. He always took the bait and ran toward us.

The aim of the game was to see who would win the charge: the sheep or the girl.

That's not to say we didn't sometimes get hurt when playing outdoors. Bronte got kicked in the face by a horse. Sierra got a fishing hook stuck in her finger. I once fell off a horse and the horse ran over me. Injuries were a regular occurrence, but my parents never responded with more rules. They knew that we would eventually learn how to keep ourselves safe and how to manage ourselves outside.

One of my more serious injuries occurred when I fell off a horse and broke my arm in multiple places. When my mum took me to the hospital, I had to get a temporary cast, and then I was scheduled for surgery two days later. They estimated it would be over twelve weeks before my arm was healed. On the drive to the hospital for the surgery, I asked my mum, "Can't God heal my arm?" She told me yes, but I was having the surgery, and with time everything would be fine when my arm healed. But I was confused; didn't we know God to be a healer? Couldn't He heal my arm now? Why should I wait twelve weeks? "Mum, I remember you saying that the same power in Jesus is also in us. So doesn't that mean I can just pray in the name of Jesus for my arm to be healed?"

She didn't need to respond because I was convicted to pray for myself. I knew that's what Elizabeth would do! I put my hand on my arm and said, "Dear Jesus, heal my arm. Thank You. Amen." When we arrived at the hospital and met with the surgeon, I asked him if he would take one more X-ray before the procedure. He was adamant about getting started right away, but I put my foot down. "I'm not going to the surgery unless you do an X-ray first." He looked at my mother, whose expression must have helped him realize

I wasn't going to change my mind and wouldn't cooperate until he did this. So he ordered a final round of X-rays.

Thirty minutes later, he came back holding the film in his hand and said to my mum, "I have no idea what happened here, but her arm is completely healed." He was wide-eyed, and I noticed a slight tremble when he held up the film. He may have had no explanation, but I wasn't the least bit surprised because God said we could be healed in His name, and He had healed me.

I would soon learn that I wasn't able to heal every time I prayed. One of my favorite pets on the farm was a fluffy baby goat we named Marshmallow. We could hear him from all over the property; he was so vocal, bleating his thoughts on this or that. We would put Marshmallow in the field with the horses, and he'd follow my pony, Charlie, around the pasture. He was so cute I would grab his face and kiss his nose while he baaed. He was such a happy little goat, jumping up on the wheelbarrow, then jumping off and kicking his legs in the air.

We'd had Marshmallow for a few months when one day, my mum packed us in the car to take us to school. We drove down our long driveway, and she stopped at the end before pulling onto the main road. I saw our trash can, and hanging out of it were Marshmallow's legs!

"Mum?"

When my mum turned around to look at me, she saw what I was staring at. In her natural bluntness and her hope to keep the situation positive, she said, "Yes, your horse killed it; Marshmallow is dead. The past is the past. Honey, move on." My mum had grown up in a family that had yet to learn the power of giving emotions the space to be processed. Since I became an adult, I've had many conversations about this with her, and I'm so proud of how she has grown in empathy.

I didn't say anything the rest of the car ride as I worked to swallow my feelings and carry on with the day. I never cried over Marshmallow. But I know Elizabeth would have.

Sometimes in our story, sadness is the hero. It took me a long time to give myself permission to stay in moments of sadness and truly feel the weight of them. When facing the hard realities of life, it is natural to feel sad. Instead of focusing on avoiding sadness, we might be surprised by how much better we feel after letting ourselves cry. It's like releasing a dam of pent-up emotions; after the tears flow, there's often a sense of relief. As I grew in my journey of courage, I realized that it takes incredible bravery to sit with sadness, to face the feeling of it, and to know that God can also heal us from emotional injuries when we bring those things to Him for healing. But He cannot heal us if we're not brave enough to admit that we are broken. It's difficult to deny the reality of a broken arm, and so in some ways, bringing that to God for healing is more straightforward. It's much easier to deny that you have a broken heart—to hide that reality from yourself, from others, and from God. It takes great courage to admit your sadness, to face it, and to ask for healing from God.

~~~

As we settled into our new life in New Zealand, my parents began testing out different churches. One church we visited, Life Church New Zealand, I instantly loved because they showed the Tarzan movie, and I had never thought I'd be able to go to church and watch a movie. Even as a little girl, I had an assertive, persuasive personality. I sat my parents down and let them know we were selecting the "Tarzan church." I wasn't too worried about their responses because I had gone to each family member beforehand and convinced them that this was our new church.

After attending this church for a few months, the children's pastor took my mum aside and said, "I'd like to talk to you about your daughter Riley. I don't know if you're aware that Riley's given her life to Jesus now for the third Sunday in a row." My mum had known about the first time I had lifted my hand and said the prayer, but she didn't realize I had done it the following two Sundays as well.

After church the next Sunday, Mum took me aside (after I'd given my life to Jesus a fourth time), and she said, "Riley, you do know you only need to give your life to Jesus once, right? Why do you keep doing it?" I'm told I turned my little seven-year-old self to her and said, "Oh, I know, Mum, but I want Jesus to know I'm serious." That has always been my relationship with Jesus. There is an unbreakable bond I've known since I was a little girl. Since I was seven or so, I've told Jesus, "I'm with You. There's no turning back." And there has been no turning back. Jesus just made sense to me.

Around this age, I started keeping a journal that I wrote in every day. The first year, I just wrote the same thing: *Jesus, You are my best friend. Please forgive me of my sins. I love You. Amen.* The pages didn't all look the same because I drew hearts and other little decorations in the margins. I have one journal with pages full of this. Occasionally, I added a new sentence, but this was the gist of it.

My mum soon took the role of kids' pastor at Life Church, and I went with her to all four services on Sundays. There was no other option in my mind. My mum got my sisters and me to be on the prayer team. At the end of the church service, people would come up front to be prayed for. In a church of ten thousand members, a lot of people came up to receive prayer. My mum would send me and my sisters out and tell us, "Girls, there's no Junior Holy Spirit; go be part of the prayer team." We'd sit on the side, looking around the crowd of people, deciding which person to pray for. Many times, we each would find our eyes landing on the same person and our hearts would choose them. My sisters and I would pull on the person's sleeve and say, "We'd love to pray for you."

My parents taught us at an early age to hear the voice of the Lord. They made it so simple. "You can hear God's voice just as clearly as you hear our voices. Have you talked to God about it?" My parents always directed us to Jesus before they'd give their own opinions. I'm sure it was difficult at times to refrain from saying what they wanted to say. But they wanted to let God speak first.

We knew that God spoke to us through an image or thought coming into our mind that was not our own. So when we prayed for people at church, why would God not speak to us about somebody else? We heard God say really specific things about people, and we shared that with them confidently. The words we spoke were almost always right on. People would often end up hysterically crying. For a long time, I thought I had magical hands because it seemed that once I put my hands on somebody and prayed over them, they'd cry.

Although I had to practice being Elizabeth in other areas of my life, when it came to my relationship with Jesus— accepting Him as my Savior, talking to Him, listening to Him, asking Him to heal my broken arm, having Him as my best friend, and pouring His love into others—I felt courage rise up within my heart. That's who Jesus was to me. He was my safe place where I could be my true self. My relationship with Him was the one area of my life where I didn't need to practice being Elizabeth. I could be exactly who I was and didn't need any masks. My pony Charlie and Jesus were the two nonjudgmental presences who accepted me as I was.

~~~

God calls us to be courageous. Courage is the ability to confront difficulties with firmness and not give up; it is having the fortitude to face hard situations and rise above them; it is acting valiantly and boldly. Courage is a virtue, a mindset, a muscle, a cognitive ability—but most of all, courage is who you can become. Our choices in life foreshadow our becomingness. You have a choice to become an "Elizabeth," the version of your future self who embodies courage. Here's the secret sauce to becomingness: change happens through your everyday choices. And a little bit of courage in your daily choices goes a long way, like baking soda in a cake.

Close your eyes and imagine yourself courageous.

What would you look like? How would you carry yourself at work, at home, out and about? How would being courageous help you handle conflict? What would you do if this was how you lived your life? Who is your Elizabeth?

We often think courage looks like charging at a lion with a spear, but one of the most courageous responses may be standing still. Before you turn to your family and friends, what if you stopped and asked God, *What do You want me to do?* Then listen to the still, small voice of God calling you into something new, into becoming a new person who makes courageous choices in the midst of the noisy world and in the privacy of your heart. Our hearts are trying to pull us into big, glorifying moments where we bow from the stage, but God is just as proud of you in the private moments where He is the only witness to your acts of courage. Will His praise be enough?

What began as me creating Elizabeth as an alter ego, a seemingly mundane decision acted out on the fields of our farm, started me down the path of choosing not to live my life in the shadows. God gave me a heart big enough to care for the world one person at a time. I realized that while Elizabeth dared to fight off the bad guys, she was also courageous in the most crucial way: she deeply cared for others. She would swing from one vine to the next, cross the rapid rivers, and fight the zombies, all to save her little sisters. Soon, I started to bring this courage into my classrooms, home, and church. Your courage persona will have moral and physical courage, but I also hope you learn that the most fulfilling way to apply courage is toward the care and consideration of others.

Each day we get the opportunity to use our mundane moments to care for the people around us. Courageously loving people is a beautiful adventure. God created you in love, by love, and for love. What if you treated every stranger as someone who is already your friend? You will never meet someone God doesn't love and Jesus wouldn't die for. Slowly, when these small moments of tender care add up, we grow into courageous, kind, loving, generous people. We become the people who make this world a little brighter, a little more hopeful. Love leaves people better than we found them.

I was fortunate to have found my inner-Elizabeth, because little did I know that in a few short years, the game of Survivors would become real life, and I'd need to fully embody her if I wanted to make it out alive.

3

The Courage to Stay

"Fear is a feeling, but courage is a choice."

The day after the 2004 tsunami, a rescue boat arrived to pick up the survivors. It's hard to describe the relief I felt when I saw that boat motor up to the shore. I just wanted to go home. I was numb to the total devastation around us, tired, hot, and trying to forget the last twenty-four hours. Because getting to the top of the mountain and holding on to my family in sheer gratitude was not where the danger ended. Nature was not done unleashing its devastation. Thousands more were about to die.

The day before, having just outrun the tsunami, we stood at the top of the cliff. I could still feel my mum's kiss on my forehead, and then she promptly shifted into take-charge mode to distract us. We had climbed to safety, and now we needed a plan. "Riley, you and Sierra go check out those huts. Bronte, stay with your dad." My mum began looking for a location where we could rest and get our bearings.

A few wooden huts dotted the perimeter of the grassy patch. Presumably, these were low-cost accommodations used by backpackers. When Sierra and I peeked into the windows, we saw each hut had a simple cot and a mini kitchen. One of the huts was unlocked, so my sister and I walked in to explore. I got so excited because someone had left Coca-Cola in the little refrigerator. We loaded up with snacks and were about to head back to the family when Sierra pulled out my dad's camcorder. He'd been carrying it around in his backpack all day. There in the hut, my sister and I started role-playing as though I was a newscaster covering the natural disaster. While mock news reporting, I looked at the camera and said that we'd just survived a tsunami. After a while, we grew bored of pretending and headed back to show Mum the snacks we'd gathered. We were later told that the backpackers staying in those huts died, swept out to sea off one of the small islands.

We stayed together as the next few hours passed. Several times I tried to look through the trees down to the beach, but then my mum would assign me a new task. My parents were protecting me from more images that they knew would haunt us. My sisters and I made friends with other children who had made it to the top of the cliff, and we played games like hide-and-seek for hours, unaware of the chaos unfolding below us.

My dad found a working radio in one of the huts, and the Thai government was giving regular updates. This is how we learned that there were multiple waves, including one that was as high as seventy-five feet—which is equivalent to a seven-story building. Earthquakes on the ocean floor are how tsunamis are created. After a significant earthquake, it's common for aftershocks to follow, which can generate additional tsunamis. We later found out that when the tsunami struck, no one saw the massive waves coming. Authorities couldn't send out an alert when the 9.1 magnitude earthquake sparked the tsunami because the country's sensor system had been hit by lightning.[1]

In the late afternoon, six hours after reaching the summit of the mountain, we were informed no more waves were coming; it was safe to return to ground level. We waited awhile longer, and then my mum and dad called us over to tell us it was time to walk back down the path to our room.

My dad grabbed my hand, and as we descended, we saw downed trees and debris littering the hillside. When we finally reached the bottom, what we saw was a nightmare. Where there had once been buildings there were now just piles of rubble. Boats were in trees, and a couple were lodged on the roof of the dining area. I remember a pickup truck that drove by, and in the bed of the truck were people covered in blood, many of whom were missing an arm or a leg. Some were wailing; some just staring.

As I held on to my dad's hand, my parents each held one of my sisters, trying to distract us from looking at the carnage. As if trying to place imaginary horse blinders over our eyes, they kept repeating, "Look at me . . . just look at me." Being a very curious person, I found this hard to do because I wanted to see what was going on.

As we took in the sights, it occurred to me for the first time that we didn't know where my aunt, cousins, and grandfather were. As we walked deeper into the fray, stepping around the wounded and lots of garbage, my mum began to shout their names. Just then, I saw a person lying in the sand that looked like my cousin, so I sprinted to her only to realize it was a dead body. And thank You, Jesus, it wasn't my cousin. My mum saw me near this corpse and shouted my name.

People walked around like zombies, looking disoriented and dazed. There were far fewer people than earlier that day. Occasionally I'd hear someone whimpering or crying, but overall, the resort was eerily quiet, especially compared to the thundering chaos of just a few hours earlier. People sat next to strangers on benches or on logs, their bodies and minds disconnected, numbed by the trauma they'd somehow survived.

My family and I continued to wander through the resort, shouting out the names of other family members. My mum, who I rarely saw cry, was in tears. She believed she'd lost them all. Given what we were seeing, it was the most practical conclusion.

After searching for an hour, my parents and I were exhausted. So much adrenaline had pumped through our bodies that we finally hit a wall and were desperate for rest. I was tired of the gut-wrenching feelings, of being sticky and sweaty, of my heart racing. I just wanted to sleep and dream I was somewhere else.

My parents eventually led us back to our apartment, and against all odds, the building was still standing. A shocking revelation was that nearly all the other structures in the resort had been damaged or wiped away, including the beachfront bungalows we'd originally planned to stay in. My dad unlocked the door and we entered our apartment.

My sisters went straight to bed, but I headed to the shower. Feeling the full effect of the events of the day, I let the water run over my hair and body. I noticed one of my arms had blood on it; I didn't know whose it was since I hadn't been hurt. I scrubbed my whole body to get every last remnant of blood and dirt and memories off me. I just wanted to be clean. When my skin was pink from scrubbing and the water running cool, I shut off the tap, dried off, and slipped on the same candy cane pj's from the day before—but I was no longer the same girl.

I was sleeping deeply, but my mum's voice invaded my dreams. She had her hands on my shoulders and she was shaking me awake. I struggled to pull myself to consciousness, but when I registered what she was saying—"We've got to go!"—I opened my eyes and looked outside and thought, *But it's still nighttime.* I climbed out of bed, practically sleepwalking to the kitchen where I heard my dad. He stood at the table, shoving supplies in a backpack. My sisters were standing by the door, disheveled and bleary-eyed, and through the fog of interrupted deep sleep, I finally heard what my dad was shouting, "Another wave! Another wave!"

I didn't know if my little body could do it all over again, but then a spike of adrenaline hit my bloodstream. We had to run again! Icy fear prickled over my body as I wondered if we would survive this time. A man just outside was waving his arms and shouting in Thai, telling us to hurry up. I rushed for the door, not changing out of my pj's or even putting on shoes. My dad threw on the backpack, my mum ushered us into the hallway, and we followed this man out of the building and away from the main beach. And yes, my father again locked the door behind us.

The Thai man led us through the streets and down alley-ways, and I realized my error in not putting shoes on. The ground was covered in metal and debris. We stopped when we reached a forest at the base of a mountain on the northern side of the peninsula, an area we were unfamiliar with. Our guide ran into the dark woods and we paused. My mum and dad looked at each other, wondering if we should follow him. We couldn't see signs of a tsunami, and the ground wasn't shaking as it had earlier. What if this was a trick?

A moment later the guide came back, waving his arms and shouting in English, "Follow me!" My parents paused, a silent conversation passing between them, and then my dad nodded and just like that we took off after the guide onto a wooded path. My feet were shattered, and at one point I hit my foot on a tree and doubled over in pain. But we had to move quickly.

We made our way up the mountain and eventually fell onto a massive grassy patch. The Thai man pointed, and we noticed others lying on the grass. He turned back to us and spoke one word: "Survivors." Oh, how far we'd come from the time when Survivors was just a game. There must have been a few hundred people there, gathered into little groups, many huddled under blankets trying to sleep. We later found out that there was no new tsunami but an abnormally high tide that had freaked everyone out.

A group of guys off to the side called the man's name. Before he rejoined his friends, he looked at us and raised his hand in salute. Then he was gone; I never saw him again. Regardless, he risked his life to help us. The most amazing thing happened next. I heard someone shouting my mum's and dad's names. There, in the middle of the grassy patch, was every single member of my extended family.

My mum and her sisters sprinted toward one another and embraced, crying and hugging. I heard my cousins shouting our names and then saw our grandfather. We later found out that one of my cousins had gone down to the main beach, and in the thirty minutes between each wave, he rescued people. He found a five-year-old boy hugging a tree, covered in dirt but somehow not hurt. Amazingly, the little boy didn't know how to swim and yet had survived the first wave. Meanwhile, the boy's parents were distraught, each thinking the other one had the boy. They were yelling at each other, so angry, clearly heartbroken. My nineteen-year-old cousin arrived, carrying their boy. When they caught sight of him holding their little boy, they ran up to him and ripped their son out of his arms. The strangest thing was, they just walked away. They never said thank you. Sometimes, doing the right thing does not translate into recognition or appreciation, but my cousin taught me that bravery is always worth it, regardless of whether it is acknowledged.

As a family, we were exhausted. We grabbed the water bottles and blankets from the backpack my dad had brought. (Amid serious threat and chaos, how he managed to be logical and practical amazes me.) Just as I was drifting off to sleep, the oddest thing happened. All of a sudden, hundreds of frogs came out of the woods and bushes and were jumping all over people. They were croaking and making noises, just singing the night away. Here we were, human and animal, all survivors of the tsunami.

It was a beautiful and memorable testimony, hearing creation sing thanks and praise, just grateful to still be alive.

~

The day after the tsunami, I woke up to my mum saying my name. A rescue boat was filling up, and I watched my extended family get on board, about to leave this devastation and begin the journey home. I leaned down to get my bag and make my way to the loading area, but my parents stopped me. My mum gently touched my arm and looked at me and my sisters. "Girls, we aren't going home just yet. Your dad and I decided we're going to stay a bit longer and help where we can."

We turned away from the retreating boat carrying our extended family—whom we'd lost and found and now were losing again—and faced the devastation before us. Boats hung in trees; buildings were piles of rubble. Along with us were about thirty others who stayed behind, most of them native Thais who either lived or worked in the resorts at Railay Beach.

My parents' response to this disaster was to help others. They've always stressed the deep value of serving. Staying in Thailand after the tsunami is the best example of what it means to have the courage to stay when everything in your mind and body wants to run—to safety, to home, to a shower and warm bed in a safe country untouched by tragedy. It takes an immense amount of courage to say, "I'm not going anywhere. Let's roll up our sleeves and get to work."

Staying was a dangerous decision for several reasons, but top of mind was not knowing when another rescue boat would return. The peninsula, only accessible by boat, was running low on food and clean water. We ate a lot of spicy rice, which was dropped off by helicopter thanks to the Thai government. There wasn't enough for us to eat our fill, so we remained hungry for several days. Residents who had lost their homes had to contend with the hazards of aggressive monkeys, unsanitary conditions, and contaminated food and water.

Scattered around were things still difficult to look at. Bodies floated in the water, and there were rumors of cholera. The ocean that had once been crystal clear was now dirty and disgusting. Someone said a shark was found in one of the nearby swimming pools.

We made our way back to the hotel room and began a pattern of how the following days would pass. Our parents went out each day and came back hours later, dirty and sweaty. My dad would tell us what he saw washed up on shore: "I found someone's watch. I saw a school of fish!" But we knew what he wasn't telling us. Still, he tried to be lighthearted and to distract us, despite spending the day clearing the debris, bodies, and rubble around the resort.

My sisters and I played in the apartment and sometimes went out to help the hotel workers clean up. One of the most haunting images in my mind was the suitcases. Groups started gathering all the suitcases found in the apartments and lined them up on the beach so that people could come and claim their personal items. Hundreds and hundreds of different-sized and colored suitcases sat in a row down the beach. Almost all of them remained unclaimed.

On day four, one of the survivors died because of food poisoning. This news made my mum and dad anxious to get back to the mainland. Staying and serving was a noble decision until the risk grew too great to overlook. Wisdom was telling them it was time to go home.

The awful-tasting rice was running low, and my sisters and I were so hungry. My parents prayed for another boat to come. We had been communicating with the government by radio. They knew we needed help, but we were just one coastal area out of hundreds that sit off the coast of Thailand, and they were overwhelmed trying to rescue people.

Finally, a boat came one week after the tsunami had struck. On that boat were volunteers from various charities, one of which was World Vision. A lady wearing an orange shirt with a World Vision logo on it jumped out of the boat and ran up to me. I don't know why she ran up to me specifically and not somebody else, but she put her arms around me and I started to cry. Tears ran down her cheeks and then she prayed for me. Here was a person who hadn't lived through this tragedy, which was such a relief to me. She hugged me and praised me for being strong. Her gesture was a perfect human response of love and care, and it's a moment I still cherish.

We got on the boat and headed back to the mainland.

~

On December 26, 2004, three tsunami waves struck, killing over 230,000 people. The "Boxing Day" tsunami devastated the coastlines of fourteen countries, making it one of the deadliest natural disasters in recorded history.[2]

It took me years to comprehend just how much courage was required for my parents to willingly stay and help when we could have gone home. My parents' conviction was strong enough to not let fear of starvation, disease, or another tsunami stop them. They cared about a cause bigger than themselves even at a significant level of risk to themselves and their children. They chose to remain in uncertainty rather than run to safety, to care for the people in a land that was not even their own.

My parents weren't responsible for the tsunami, but they took responsibility for the damage the tsunami caused. How can we take responsibility for something that isn't ours? When we find the courage to stay, we oppose the bystander effect, which says that when many people are watching, it becomes even harder to do what we know is right because we tend to do what others are doing. We assume someone else will step in to help. It's easier to look the other way when we see a stranger in trouble.

Imagine how healing it would be for society if we each went against the bystander effect. We can choose not to watch from a distance but to push up our sleeves and get involved, to get messy and dirty. My parents returned to our apartment each day after laboring with strangers, covered in sweat and dirt, but smiling. There's something profound about the deeply rewarding feeling that comes from serving, which boosts our self-respect.

On a trip to South Africa a few years later, I heard the word "ubuntu" used in conversation several times. Ubuntu is a culturally common word that means we are all connected in some way. There is an African legend about an anthropologist who went to Nigeria and one day was playing with a group of kids. He put a basket of fruit near a tree and said whoever could run to the tree the fastest would get to eat the fruit. When he said "Run!" the children all held hands and took off running together. When they reached the tree, they all sat down and began to eat the sweet treats. He asked them why they ran together instead of alone—the winner would have had all that fruit to themselves. They said, "How can one of us be happy if all the others are sad?" "Ubuntu" means "I am because we are" in the Xhosa culture.[3] My parents were modeling what ubuntu looks like after the tsunami struck, but I also saw them live into this word in their everyday lives.

~

Once the rescue boat arrived on the mainland, we taxied to the airport. It was finally time to go home. Sections of the airport had been turned into a makeshift hospital with beds set up for displaced and injured people. We passed several people who were bloody and bruised and in terrible pain. The hospitals were overwhelmed. Some had survived the tsunami but were now slowly dying due to the lack of proper medical care. I tried to breathe through my mouth because the smell was so bad that I was afraid I might get sick.

The airport had also become a hub for survivors, a place where people went to find their missing loved ones. Nearly a quarter of a million people had died, but thousands of people were still missing.[4] We were lucky to have found our extended family within a day. Others had been looking for missing people for a week at this point.

At one end of the airport was a wall that had been covered with white paper where people could write the names of their missing loved ones. I saw thousands and thousands of names on that wall. I watched as a man and woman scrutinized each name. They just kept hunting for a name they weren't finding. Down the line a bit was another man, going the opposite direction, studying the names and moving slowly. As the couple and this man made their way down the wall, they got closer and closer to each other. Finally, they were close enough that their shoulders touched. They each turned to look at the person beside them and froze. They were looking at the face of the person whose name they were searching for. They grabbed each other in a tight hug, crying and laughing. We learned that this couple had just gotten married, and the other individual was their best man! They had spent an entire week in Thailand for the wedding and imagined they'd lost one another.

My family and I watched this encounter, and then we heard our names being called over the intercom. It was time to board the plane to Bangkok and then off to New Zealand.

My friend, I may have faced a tsunami, but so have you. You have faced the unexpected and difficult, whether that was being bullied, losing someone, abuse, or a traumatic event. In each of our lives, it's not *if* a tsunami will come; it's *when* a tsunami will come. The question we then ask ourselves is, *How will we respond?*

We are most often not in control of the hardships that hit our lives, but we are responsible for the way we respond. We can choose to cower in fear or freeze in indecision. Or we can choose to rise up: fear is a feeling, but courage is a choice.

An easy life is an exception; a hard life is the rule. When the hardships of life come, we quickly learn who we truly are. We can become a diamond, something more beautiful and precious because it has been tried under heat and pressure and been transformed. God can take the hard stuff in our lives and make us stronger. He can turn our messes into a message and a test into a testimony.

I think of my cousin who put himself in danger by going back down the mountain to rescue anyone he saw. He could have easily stayed at the top in safety, but he chose not to.

His choice has impacted me, but not only me. The beauty of choosing to help is the ripple effect on the people around us. Like dominoes lined up in a row, when we go against the bystander effect and step forward to help another person, that courage touches someone else who then is inspired to help someone, and eventually people we may never meet are impacted by our initial choice to help.

Fifty percent of Jesus's miracles were disruptions—times when he was on his way to somewhere else to see someone else but was interrupted by someone in need. He wasn't afraid of being late or even of offending other people because he saw the need of the person in front of him. These "holy disruptions" happen when we're willing to be inconvenienced for the sake of someone else.

Think of situations when the harder or costlier choice is to stay. Maybe it's staying with a friend who drinks too much at a party or choosing to chat with an elderly person who is lonely or staying an extra day with your family at Thanksgiving. We are given opportunities every day to care for others. Will you find just one person to care about today?

Life is short. It may seem impossible to imagine yourself no longer being alive, but it is one guarantee we can't avoid. Death doesn't discriminate; it comes for everyone. As the poet Mary Oliver asks, "Tell me, what is it you plan to do with your one wild and precious life?"[5] And God gave you this life. So think about this: While you're here and able, how will you use the beautiful gift of your life? I hope you choose to participate in things that will last far longer than your years here on earth. Care for the people around you who are in need. Your courage needs to touch only one life for the ripple effect to begin. If you change one person, you can change the world.

4

The Battle between Fear and Courage

"I was living a fractured life."

In my dream, I had tensed every muscle in my body in preparation for the tsunami that was about to break over me. Trapped beneath the weight of the water, I flailed my arms and legs, trying to find the surface. I woke to the sound of shattering glass. When I opened my eyes, I saw the lamp that had been on my nightstand now in pieces on the floor. I leaped out of bed, wide-eyed and panting. *Where am I?*

My mum rushed into the room and grabbed my shoulders. "It's okay, honey, it's okay." I held on to her, trembling. When my breathing returned to normal, she wiped the hair off my forehead and looked me in the eye. "Riley, I want you to say something every single time you have a nightmare . . . every single time you feel overwhelmed. I want you to say, 'The peace of God that transcends all understanding, guard my heart and mind in Christ Jesus.'"[1] Even all these years later, I still occasionally have nightmares about the tsunami, and without fail, I repeat those words my mum gave me.

~

When the plane touched down in New Zealand and we reentered our former life, we were bombarded by people who wanted to hear our story—at school, in the supermarket, and at church. People heard about us on the news, and we were well known now as "the family from New Zealand who had survived the tsunami."

At first, this was exciting because I love people and I love attention. Now the girl with only a few friends was the "cool" person. We attended a church of ten thousand people, and my mum was one of the pastors. I remember a few old ladies coming up to me one of the first Sundays after we'd gotten home. They tapped me on my shoulder and asked to hear my story.

People love a story of hope, as they should, but I felt pressure to present myself as joyful each time I recounted the story. I saw in people's eyes and their facial expressions how much they enjoyed hearing about how my family had survived. So I told it joyfully, and I told it with hope. I made sure to end on a positive note because if I had shared how I truly felt or what had truly happened, I thought it would be too shocking for them. It would change the story from hopeful to traumatizing. Some details I will never share. No ten-year-old girl—in fact, no one—should see a man violently thrown into a pounding wave.

I didn't have the resources to express the sadness I felt in those first weeks and months back at home. If I'm really honest, my joy was a protective mechanism; it was a shield from deeper vulnerability. I found it far easier to act joyful and happy because I was familiar with those emotions. The cost of telling anyone that I was suffering felt too high, and I simply wasn't mature enough to express it at age ten or for many years after.

After school, even if the sun was shining, I put on my gum boots and rain jacket and ran out to meet our animals. I'd throw my arms around my pony, Charlie's, neck. He had this amazing ability to hug a person back by turning his head so that it wrapped around a person's shoulders. He'd stay there until I let go. I like to imagine he sensed how badly I needed a hug. Charlie had no agenda, no expectation of me, no words—he simply provided a quiet presence. And it was just what I needed.

I spent time with Charlie almost every day after school, crying, telling him about my day, and sharing my feelings. Then I would take a deep breath, go back into the house, and act joyful and strong again. But Charlie knew the truth.

The discrepancy between how I felt and how I acted revealed something about myself that I didn't like. It doesn't feel good when your emotions don't match your lived experience. Imagine having a fractured leg and walking around trying to hide your limp. I would tell others I was doing well, but on the inside, I was crying for help. Do you ever do this? Is there a difference between what you say and how you feel? Have you shared how you're really feeling with close friends?

I once met a man in a coffee shop who told me, "I have two goals in life: one, to die with no secrets, and two, to never lie to myself." This man knew that if we aren't genuine, we can never be vulnerable and honest, which keeps us from growing and creating true connections with one another and with God.

Masking our true feelings is risky. We risk the opportunity to know the Lord, who, by the way, does not require perfection from us. God wants our presence, not our perfection. God accepts us as we are. There is nothing you've felt that makes God look away. He is not ashamed of you. But when we are inauthentic, we close ourselves off from Him and His help.

My need to tell our family's story joyfully had its origin in a few sources. One was that our family's reputation felt important. Even before the tsunami, my parents were well known in our community. My dad ran big companies, and my mum was a pastor at the largest church in New Zealand. When I walked into coffee shops or went to public places, people knew who I was. My parents sometimes made remarks to us about our reputation, not in an oppressive or unhealthy way, but we knew it was important to think about how we presented ourselves to others.

Another source of the pressure I felt came from wanting to honor my family. New Zealand culture is an honor-shame culture, in which a person's words and actions bring honor or shame to their family. It's very different from American culture where people tend to make decisions based on individual preference. In New Zealand, people make decisions after asking themselves two questions: *How will this affect me? How will this affect my family or community?*

It is a lot of tension for a young girl to hold, and it's clear to me now that in those first days, weeks, and months back in New Zealand, I was struggling with PTSD. I needed time to adjust to reality after a near-death experience and help in dealing with my feelings of sadness and restlessness. Large chunks of time during that first year are lost in my memory, as if they've been erased. Part of this lack of memory is because I was young, but forgetfulness is also a natural response to trauma.

I was living a fractured life. I maintained an outward identity that wasn't entirely false, but which didn't reveal the whole truth of my feelings, and an interior identity where I could be my true self. This imbalance delayed the healing process for me. Dear reader, don't do what I did and delay your own healing. Maybe you know the mismatch of feelings when you're drowning on the inside but smiling on the outside. When we are authentic in sharing how we feel, we can start to heal.

But it doesn't end there. Some trauma takes a lifetime to process. I'm okay with giving myself all the time I need. Imagine me handing you a slip of paper that grants you permission to take the time you need to process and heal from your trauma. I've processed my trauma on a couch in a therapy room, at a table with my mentor, on a kitchen floor with my best friend, and even on a first date with a cute man. (I don't recommend the latter!) It takes time, often years, and safe places to retell our painful events until they no longer feel painful.

If I could tell my ten-year-old self one thing, I'd let her know she did her best dealing with her trauma. She didn't know better and wasn't taught a better way. I'd grab her in a big hug so she felt like she was hugging Charlie and whisper, "It's okay to be sad." Oddly enough, I'd tell my twenty-two-year-old self the same thing. It wasn't until then that I broke down crying in a coffee shop after my spiritual mentor asked me three times, "No, Riley, how do you really feel about the tsunami?" That is when I finally approached my story authentically. I could finally tell the story in a way that lined up with how I felt inside.

I don't think I allowed myself to feel what I considered "bad" emotions—anger, sadness, or anxiety—because I worried those feelings were sinful. Now I know that no emotion is inherently bad, and having strong emotions isn't sinful. It's what we choose to do with those emotions that matters.

Our emotions are a gift from God, and it is good for us to feel them. Just saying out loud how we're feeling can be very freeing. When I was acting joyful, I was allowing myself to experience only one emotion, which had me seeing the world in black and white. But when I allowed in other emotions such as sadness, anger, and disappointment, I was able to view the world in color.

For the first twenty years of my Christian walk, I pushed down difficult emotions, believing they were incompatible with faith. However, the Bible paints a different picture. King David, considered a man after God's own heart, openly expressed a vast range of feelings before the Lord— two-thirds of his psalms are filled with lamentations and complaining! The prophet Jeremiah penned an entire book dedicated to his profound grief over Jerusalem's destruction. Even Jesus didn't shy away from expressing anger and sadness.

Neuroscientists have found that if we grow up in families where emotions are not openly expressed, it can hinder the development of certain parts of our brain.[2] This, in turn, affects our ability to love and work effectively. However, the good news is that this damage is not permanent. Research has also revealed that our brains can rewire themselves when we learn to acknowledge and label our emotions.[3]

You can begin to name your feelings by writing in a journal as part of your time with God. You might prayerfully consider and respond to questions such as the following:

What am I feeling right now? Why am I feeling sad/lonely/angry/worried?

Where in my body am I holding stress? Do I feel the tension in my shoulder, back, gut, and so on?

Are there any lies I am believing about myself or others? Pray and ask God what the truth is.

Is what I'm feeling helping me or hurting me?

What is God calling me to do with the emotions I'm feeling?

When you are honest with God about your anger or sadness, you will meet a God who is delighted to give you freedom. Ignored or misnamed emotions always find a way to come out, and usually those ways aren't healthy or helpful. If pain is not transformed, it is transmitted. Many addictions arise from a place of unhealed trauma, a lack of safe places to simply "be," and denied emotions.

Fear kept me from sharing my true feelings. It took me years to reframe the experience and share my story without being afraid.

~~

Although it would take me a long time to embrace my full range of emotions about the tsunami, there was mercy in my immediate, newfound appreciation for life. My experience developed in me a deep gratitude for the little things. When we have close encounters with death, we realize how much we truly want to live.

When we got back home after the tsunami, time seemed to move so slowly. But a flower on the ground or a little baby laughing would remind me of just how happy I was to be alive. Each new day was a blank canvas of possibility and life—and I felt determined to scribble all over it. I wrote in my journal most nights, listing all that I was grateful for: the stars, Charlie, chocolate, my favorite English teacher who nicknamed me "Smiles," and my best friend, Sam.

Even though it wasn't healthy to always focus on only the positive side of what my family went through, God still met me in my suffering and taught me many valuable lessons. I learned that suffering is an invitation into deeper intimacy with the Lord because when we suffer, we discover that God is the only One we can fully rely on. No human is as reliable as God. I also learned the comforting truth that as a follower of Christ, our suffering is limited to this life only (see Rev. 21:4). And I learned that in suffering, we will have the opportunity to test, try, and prove our courage. Courage too is needed on this side of heaven only.

When we are in the battle of our lives, each of us will have (or has had) a "destiny moment." We will have the option to bring value out of our suffering. Like a soldier's obedience to a commander's order, we trust the Lord to create good from the suffering as we welcome Him into it. That destiny moment comes when we look death in the face and realize we could lose everything. In the pressing in, we get honest and learn what we're made of, who we are, and who we want to become.

My destiny moment came after the tsunami, when I had my little hands wrapped around Charlie's fluffy neck and decided I wanted to be for other people what Charlie was for me: a safe place for people living through their own tsunamis.

I chose to commit to helping others, even when I felt like curling up into a ball of fear. In the depth of suffering, there is an invitation to something greater. In Jesus's life, it was through His greatest suffering that we were set free.

In addition to feeling immense gratitude for being alive, another positive outcome of the tsunami was the impact it had on my relationship with Jesus. I wondered why God let me live when I had watched thousands of people die. I didn't dwell there—it wasn't in my personality to question, and I sure wasn't going to question Him! So while I didn't understand it, I chose to trust that He had a reason. More than ever, I saw God as my protector and thought about how He is able to not only run the entire world but also see every event, every heart.

Six months after the tsunami, my parents bought a dingy vacation house overlooking a beach (high up on a mountain so that if a tsunami happened to hit the coast of New Zealand, we would survive) in Tairua, a quaint beach town located on North Island of New Zealand. For our summer holiday, we packed the car, loaded the horses in the trailer, and went to our vacation house. I was so excited because school was out!

A few days before the start of summer break, my parents told me and my sisters they had enrolled us in a beach lifeguarding program. We would begin training in a few days. *Beach lifeguarding, they've got to be kidding*, I thought. As in, train every day at the very place I was now desperately afraid of? This brought about a series of feelings beginning with shock and then anger. Next, my stubbornness reared up. It felt so unjust to force us to go into the ocean.

My greatest fear was the ocean—and with good reason. I had watched the ocean kill countless people. The sight still haunts me to this day. Some of us are born with fears, and others can pinpoint the origin of their fear. The tsunami was my fear's origin story.

It is vital to note that our fears can be either normative or from trauma, and sometimes they're a mix of both. I was afraid of the ocean and had nightmares and flashbacks in response to a traumatic event. Maybe you can relate to living through something incredibly frightening, and as a result, you experience the symptoms as if the event were happening again and again. This is a different sort of fear from how I felt standing before my classmates to speak, being near my bullies, or even being near the boy I had an unspoken crush on. These feelings are normal, coming-of-age fears. Despite the difference between these types of fear, both are worth facing and overcoming so that you can live more freely and confidently.

What is *your* fear? What is your *worst* fear? What is your greatest fear in life *right now*? I want you to think about this for a minute. Maybe it is tarantulas, heights, being stuck in a tight space, or being alone. Maybe your fear takes the form of anxiety or depression.

Now think of your greatest fear and imagine, for a second, being forced to face it. How would you feel?

On the first day of beach lifeguard training, I was absolutely terrified. I'd never nervous-peed so many times in my life. That morning, I didn't eat anything, and I'd had very little the day before because I was so nervous. My stomach growled and churned, and my heart kicked up a faster beat. The night before I'd had a nightmare. While my parents helped us get ready, they acted as if it was just another day. I couldn't believe they were going to force me to do this! My sisters felt the same way.

I put on my swimsuit and looked at myself in the mirror. I was pale and my hair was a mess. Ten minutes before it was time to leave, I went down to the kitchen where my dad was. He picked up on the fact that I was not okay. What came next was one of the most important moments of my life. He pulled me over to the corner of the kitchen and put both hands on my shoulders. "Riley, either courage or fear will exist in your life, and you get to choose which one wins. All you need is a little more courage." I never forgot what he told me. These words echoed in my heart, and I still hear them to this day. They gave me language for how I wanted to live my life.

I've read that the name "Riley" evolved from the Gaelic word for valiant,[4] and I wanted my name to represent this new call to courage, to be "valiantageous"—a word I made up to mean so valiant, so courageous, that it was contagious. This is what I wanted to be. It was the beginning of years of learning to become not Elizabeth but Riley, my own name.

We piled into the car. My sisters and I were silent, staring off into oblivion like zombies while my parents chatted. The two-minute drive down to the beach felt way longer.

In the area near our beach house, lifeguarding was a common summertime job for kids over fourteen. For younger kids, it was a summer program. This got kids out of the house and gave parents a chance to relax. The parking lot was full of smiling, energetic children of all ages. I took in all their excitement, but I couldn't match it. My parents walked us over to a table to check in, all the while talking to people here and there while my sisters and I followed obediently, not making a sound. They separated us into three different lines for the three different squads based on age.

As I stood at the back of the line with all the other kids my age, I remained quiet. Unsure of what to say or feel, I was relieved when a blonde, blue-eyed girl named Rosie walked up and wanted to be friends. She quickly realized I wasn't feeling talkative, but she just chatted away. Rosie became really important to me that summer. She seemed to understand I was going through something, but she didn't press me to talk about it and she didn't expect me to change. She stayed by my side and encouraged me when all the other kids were swimming or running faster, even though she was the fittest girl in the squad. She'd stay back with me.

Three weeks into training, I was still in a constant battle between courage and fear. Most days, it felt like fear was winning. I'd repeat my dad's words, "a little more courage," to give me inspiration. Something I learned that summer is that the more you face your fear, the less power it has over you.

One day, stormy weather blew in; the waves were huge, and riptides circled in the water. We were instructed to swim out to a buoy life ring located three hundred feet from the shore. As I was swimming, a massive wave crashed over me, pulling me under and spinning me around. When I finally broke the surface of the water, I gasped for air and looked around. Terrified but determined to get to the buoy, I kept swimming. When I got back on shore, Rosie rushed over to me. "Are you okay? You don't look well." I told her about the wave, but didn't share any details.

"Riley, next time that happens," she said, "open your eyes under the wave and you'll see just how beautiful it is." So the next time I was out in the waves I tried it, and she was right! This became a life lesson for me. Keeping my eyes closed kept me lost in my own little world filled with fear. But I could choose to open my eyes when I was scared. I could do the opposite of what fear wanted me to do. When I did so, it not only reversed my instinct to hide but also allowed me to see something beautiful that I otherwise would have missed. Underneath the waves, the water is crystal clear. I saw a variety of colorful fish swimming. I noticed the design of the sand patterns at the bottom. Even the churning water of the wave created bubbles and swirling water that brought about a sense of wonder.

Now one of my mantras whenever I feel scared and want to shut my eyes is to tell myself to keep my eyes open and catch the beauty.

~

When I was thirteen years old, my parents moved me from a small coed Christian school to a large all-girls private school in New Zealand called Diocesan School for Girls ("Dio" for short). The school property had manicured gardens and austere brick buildings. We wore floor-length, formal skirts and blazers. Very posh. Our family wasn't at the same level of wealth as the typical student at Dio. A large part of my tuition was paid by a scholarship. My peers had elevators in their city homes, while my dad once fell through the roof of our farmhouse because it was moldy.

Every year, I always was a little bit of an outsider at school largely because my partial deafness was isolating. Also, Jesus was my best friend and that made me stand out. I was so passionate about Jesus that I would stand on the wooden tables during lunchtime, share the gospel with students, and lead an altar call. This did not help my position in the social pecking order!

I ran around helping everyone I could. I went into "serving overdrive." I see now that service allowed me to pay attention to something other than the grief and sadness raging inside of my own heart. To this day, when I get in the overdoing-it mode, it's clear to me that I'm avoiding some emotion—a completely unproductive endeavor. Nevertheless, I'll start calling my friends and telling them I love them, signing up to volunteer somewhere, or starting a new club—running around like a mouse on a wheel thinking I'm going somewhere. I started or ran seven different clubs, from Bible studies to SADD (Students Against Drunk Driving) to "Save the Whales." One night, I heard about beached whales and cried so hard that my mum got worried. I decided to do something about it. When I thought of a chunky, sad whale stranded on a beach, I was motivated into action, even if others couldn't understand or thought I was a weirdo. So I put up posters all around the cafeteria for the first "Save the Whales Club" meeting.

I expected one person to show up, but my mouth dropped open when thirty other students piled into the classroom. We ended up having the time of our lives and raised enough money to buy a life-size inflatable whale so that people could practice how to help beached whales.

Surviving an event that a lot of people didn't survive created a new voice in my head. It told me I would need to work to pay back God for saving my life. I thought, *He spared my life, so I owe Him the rest of my life.* The curse of this lie is that the debt never seemed to decrease with each good thing I did. No matter how many acts of love I showed, I never felt like I had done enough. I wanted to "do" and "work" for God, like His little employee. But God does not want commandership; He wants partnership with us. He doesn't need us to be the hero. He doesn't need us to fix everybody and everything. He loves me, and He loved my little heart that wanted to help everybody. But at the same time, He has clearly said to me, "Rest in Me, Riley," or "Be still, and know that I am God" (Ps. 46:10).

I've learned how to hush the voice that told me I owed God, because the reality is there is no debt to pay back. Christ paid a debt that humankind owed, but He doesn't expect us to pay Him back. God isn't expecting me to pay Him back for saving me in Thailand. This idea has haunted my life—even to this day, it occasionally shows up and I have to wrestle with it again. I am grateful to be alive, and I choose to make my life count to the maximum effect. It's the least I can do. I can do as many good deeds as possible as an act of gratitude to God, but I have to maintain a balance. It would be such an insult to God's grace for me to live through a tsunami and then spend the rest of my life on the couch eating potato chips and binge-watching movies. Though even if I did choose to do that for the rest of my life, God would still love me!

I was also wrong in thinking that I needed to be in overdrive, helping others and sharing God's love at a frantic pace because time was short. He's not expecting that from me, and I know from experience, it only leads to burnout. I try to be mindful of living a healthy, balanced life. I want to make my life a gift to others for the sake of the gospel but not at the expense of time with my family, friends, community—and myself.

At school, I felt myself being drawn to students I hadn't noticed before. The other gift of surviving the tsunami was a new level of empathy for those who seemed lonely, broken, or hurt. I started to actively seek out students who sat alone at lunch or classmates who acted like outsiders. As a result of this effort, I became known as the "unofficial school counselor." My parents told me, "Riley, go be a sneaky ninja for Jesus," meaning, do acts of kindness without recognition. My favorite kind act was to write encouraging letters to girls who looked sad, signed "Love, your secret angel," and sneak the letters into their backpacks.

My friend, the shadows of your life have their purpose. The dark hours of sorrow and pain bring their own rich satisfaction because when you have passed through trouble, you are equipped by your own experience to sympathize with others who live in the shadows.

Once I met a girl named Genevieve whose parents were going through a divorce. She told me she was harming herself. During morning tea, she would sit and tell me about how she was truly feeling. She was so honest with her feelings, it allowed me to privately acknowledge my own true emotions. Other people's feelings can be a mirror into our own soul. Genevieve helped me understand my unnamed feelings. Her vulnerability bred my own vulnerability, and slowly, what I wrote in my journal began to express a hint of my true feelings.

I was providing a safe space for others to share what I was unable to express. I was healing through their sharing of their own pain and allowing me to walk with them through it. This was a gift from the Lord. I tucked away my deeper feelings until I was older and had the resources to properly process them, but in the meantime, I began healing through others.

I spent a year *acting* joyful after the tsunami, but after that first year, my joy became authentic, due in no small part to being able to help so many others by providing them a safe space. I would not have been so driven that early in life had I not endured that trauma. When we got home, I was purposeful in everything I did because I felt like I was on borrowed time.

Destiny is a gift that comes with the awareness of death—emphasis on *gift* because for any of us to be alive is all grace. Destiny simply means that you have been given the gift of a future—not because you are more "deserving" of one or have somehow earned it but simply by the grace of God. After the tsunami, I was no longer ignorant and could not deny the fact that death is a threat every single day. Ironically, once that thought sank in, it made me live more freely. When we keep our own mortality in a healthy perspective, we can release living for tomorrow and start living in the now.

There are two ways to ride a roller coaster. You can shut your eyes and hold on for dear life, or you can raise your arms, open your eyes, and embrace the twists and turns. On the roller coaster of life, be the one who doesn't miss the moment. As my friend Rosie taught me, choose to open your eyes and find the beauty in your life.

5

The Beauty of Vulnerability

"You hear about people having 'blind faith,'
but I had something like 'deaf trust.'"

Life is a constant practice in "a little more courage." Showing courage gets easier as you get more comfortable with being vulnerable. In fact, the quality of your life is directly linked with how much vulnerability you can handle. As a child, I wasn't one to shy away from it, even when I encountered unfriendly people. Let's be honest, some of the people I encountered were downright vicious. Let me tell you about a girl in school named Mary.

The Diocesan School for Girls, or Dio, is for grades six through twelve, but I began in the seventh grade after many of the friend groups had been established. As a new student, I was assigned a "buddy" whose job was to help me find my classes and introduce me to teachers—basically to help me get settled. My buddy's name was Mary. Her job may have been to make me feel comfortable, but that was the last thing on her mind. She was much taller than me, wore a tight ponytail with tons of gel, and had a pointy nose and dark eyes. I was so intimidated by her! I was a late bloomer, so here I was, a short, flat-chested little girl, eager to have my buddy calm some of my anxiety. Instead, Mary took it upon herself to make me feel as uncomfortable as possible.

She walked me to class but sometimes she was late, so I'd go in and save her a seat. It didn't matter where I sat—in the back, the front, or the middle—she would say it was her seat and push me off the chair if I didn't pop up immediately and move. Any seat I was in was her seat.

She also started spreading rumors and calling me names. I hadn't made any other friends yet; she was the only person I knew at this new school. Each afternoon when the bell rang at the end of the school day, I sprinted out to my mum's car that was parked in the pickup line. I'd slam the door and say, "Go, Mum, drive!" and once we got far enough away, I'd start crying. Why did I have to leave the small Christian school where I had friends, where I could hang out with boys and do things I wanted to do? I felt like an outsider.

Day after day my mum listened to me share what Mary was doing. Mary's tactics only seemed to get harsher with time. One night, my mum sat me down and said, "Riley, the next time Mary comes up to you and tries to take your seat, pinch her underneath her arm and tell her, 'Get your fat butt away from my chair. This is my seat!'" She said it in a joking way, then stopped smiling. "But, seriously, daughter, you need to fight back."

Something in what she was suggesting didn't feel right to me, though, so at the end of the day I went to my room, got down on my knees, and prayed. *God, I feel so uncomfortable at school. Mary keeps bullying me and I don't know how to handle it.* I heard the Lord respond and knew what I had to do.

The next day I asked my mum to drop me at school a little early. The last thing she said as I was leaving the car was, "Remember, Riley, fight back! Enough is enough." I nodded my head.

Near the school was a dairy, what Americans call a convenience store. I had a little bit of pocket money saved up, so I walked over and bought the nicest box of chocolates I could find. When first period was about to begin, I found my seat, and a minute later, Mary came in. She spotted me and started walking over. This time, I was ready for her. When she got to my seat, I jumped up before she could say anything, put my hand in my backpack, pulled out the box of chocolates, and said, "Mary, I bought this for you. And I also want to say something." I put my hand on her shoulder and looked her in the eye. "I know you are sometimes mean to me because somebody's been mean to you, and I hope you feel loved right now."

She looked at me, wide-eyed, and the angry expression melted away. I watched as her eyes filled with tears. Then, just as swiftly, her expression hardened again. "Get off my chair." She sat down and didn't acknowledge me for the rest of the class. Sometimes our courage leads us into vulnerable situations that feel painful. But my act of kindness wasn't discounted just because she didn't respond well.

I was so disheartened because I was sure that one gesture would break through her hard exterior and make her feel loved. I couldn't figure out what had gone wrong. Hadn't the Lord told me to do this?

Then, before our final class, Mary approached me in an empty hallway, tears in her eyes, and said, "Riley, I walk myself home every day. My parents never pick me up after school. They are going through a divorce and my mum throws plates at my dad. They scream at each other. They call each other mean names, and they call me mean names. And that's why I'm mean to you." This was the day I learned how my own vulnerability could bring out the vulnerability in another person. It's a risk because you never know how someone will respond, but in this instance, Mary felt safe exposing her family's secret to me because I had shown her that I cared. Suddenly, the hurt and anger I felt toward her shifted into empathy.

Loving another leaves us vulnerable. There is no safe investment. In any act of love, you give someone the power to hurt you. But vulnerability is a superpower because it has the ability to break down the walls of people's hearts, to get to the softness hidden behind the exterior shell. What if the next time you are hurt, you think, *What must have happened to this person for them to treat me like this?* before you jump into defense mode? Or what if you asked yourself, *How can I respond in love?* This vulnerability is a beautiful gift to others. Trust me, people connect more with your vulnerability than your ability.

I thought about how I got to leave school every day and come home to a place where my parents truly loved each other. My family laughed a lot. We danced in the kitchen to old songs my parents loved, like "Fly Me to the Moon" by Frank Sinatra. My mum was always on time to pick me up from school, waiting outside in the car line to hear all the little, and sometimes silly, details of my day. I didn't tell Mary this, but Mum always brought me a snack for the ride home. I had no idea what it felt like to be Mary and have her homelife, but Jesus did.

Maybe you have a Mary in your life right now. Someone who treats you unfairly. Someone who gossips behind your back. Someone who seems driven to destroy you. Maybe it's a work colleague who is out to beat you to the next promotion. Or a family member whose words aim to bring you down. Or a friend who secretly competes with you on beauty or fashion. Or a guy in your class who keeps making cruel remarks about your glasses or hair.

What if you had the courage to be a little more vulnerable with your Mary? Instead of responding in kind, what if next time, you respond in love? With "a little more courage" to put our vulnerabilities on display, our weaknesses can be an opportunity for a deeper connection with others and for God to show His strength in our lives.

Our hearts are like rooms. Some people have well-lit hearts; others are dark and scary. Here is the bright side: when you shine the light of love into someone else's room, the darkness is forced to flee. Even if darkness has dominated a room for months or years, it has no option but to submit to the light.

Bullies are like scared kids in a dark room, desperately searching for the light switch. They act out in cruelty because they are scared. Their actions or words are attempts to cover fear. A lit candle in a bright room causes a subtle change, but lighting a candle in a dark room is dramatic. Dark hearts provide greater opportunities for transformation. The people who are the most unlovable are the people who need love most. You can be the light in the room of someone's heart, even if it's just for a split second.

A week before I gave Mary the box of chocolates, her parents had announced their divorce. Meanwhile, the same night, my dad tucked me into bed and kissed me on the forehead. Before shutting the door, he turned around and told me, as he always did, "Riley, you are beautiful, smart, and special." Mary didn't have people shining light into her heart. She wasn't bombarded with love on a daily basis.

So before you judge the Mary in your life, thank God for them. You may be thinking, *Why, Riley, would I be thankful for the person who tries to make my life a living hell?* You should be thankful because God is giving you an opportunity to grow your light and your vulnerability. God placed them in your life for a reason, for a blessing or a lesson. You may be the only person willing to turn on the light of love in their heart. Please fumble your way through their darkness and turn on that switch.

~

God didn't spare me from having a weakness. For the first six years of my life, my parents didn't know I had a hearing impairment. They just thought I was a late developer or being disobedient. A few times, my parents even disciplined me for not obeying, and I was so confused by this. I didn't know I'd done something wrong. I simply hadn't heard them.

One day when I was six years old, my mum picked me up from kindergarten. I was walking ahead of her, and she called out to me, telling me that I needed to clean up my room when I got home. When I didn't acknowledge her, she called out to me again. "Riley, you're not showing honor right now." She finally caught up with me and put her hand on my shoulder. "Hey, when you get home, clean up your toys." I didn't know why she was using a stern tone, but I looked at her and said, "Okay yeah, sure, I will."

Later that week, we went to church and I was speaking to an elderly lady. She told me my hair was really pretty—I have massive curly hair that pops out everywhere—and she asked me my name. I could read her lips, and I told her my name. I read her lips as she repeated my name back to me, but she kept saying "Wylie" with a W, and I kept telling her no. I was getting frustrated. Why couldn't she say my name? She was probably wondering why I couldn't say my own name correctly. I was so mad I left her awkwardly standing there with no idea what was going on and ran back to my mum, hysterically crying.

Meanwhile, in school, other kids couldn't understand what I was saying even though I was trying my very best to articulate all my words. It was so confusing because, in my head, I was saying all the words correctly, but their responses made no sense. Language is essential to how we communicate and understand each other. Yet my speech was distorted because of my hearing. (My teachers—who no doubt had experience with little kids mispronouncing words—were somewhat better at understanding me.)

I didn't understand why other kids didn't want to play with me. My little sister Sierra was my hero when I was in primary school because she would follow me around on the playground and speak on my behalf. Or I would say something, and she would translate it to the other kids. Finally, with her help, I started making friends. This made me so happy! I love people and want to be everyone's friend. The bell would sound for playtime, and I'd run up to my sister, grab her hand, and we'd bounce around the playground chatting and swinging and climbing on the monkey bars. So even though I felt misunderstood when in the classroom, I never dragged my feet about going to school because time on the playground, with my sister's help, allowed me time with my friends, and that was my number one priority in life.

We were in California when I was in kindergarten, and on most Sunday nights, my grandma would call us from New Zealand, but I struggled to hear her. Communicating in a way that others could understand became such an issue that I began refusing to come to the phone to talk to my own grandma. My mum couldn't understand what was going on, but those conversations were painful. I'd say something to Grandma, she'd repeat it multiple times, and I'd get frustrated because she didn't understand me and I didn't understand her.

It wasn't until the summer after kindergarten that I got an ear infection from spending so much time in the ocean. We went to the doctor, and he discovered I was partially deaf. He asked my parents, "How's it been parenting your daughter who's partially deaf?" They looked at my doctor in shock. Turns out, I heard sounds as though I were wearing permanent noise-canceling headphones. The doctor inserted grommets, which are tiny tubes put into the eardrum that allow air to pass through and equalize the air pressure, and that helped, but hearing was still tough.

My mum and dad had to change their parenting style so that every time they talked to me, they were looking directly at me so that I could read their lips.

Not being able to hear made me feel like an outsider. My speech was slurred, and as I said, I couldn't even pronounce my own name correctly. Kids had classified me as a loner, but I was anything but that. It seemed the doors to the classrooms were always in the back of the class, and most kids would just pile in and sit in the back rows, but I had to do that walk of shame all the way to the front and find a seat. My teachers filled my report cards with comments like "Riley is stubborn and doesn't always follow instructions." I'd started horseback riding and my pony club teacher would have to use a megaphone to tell me things. It was so embarrassing.

Once I started making friends, during morning tea time (what Americans call recess), we would sit outside on the playground, and even with my sister around, I had no idea what everyone was talking about. Between the wind and laughter and voices talking over each other, the background noise made it impossible for me to hear. I seemed like a bad friend who didn't care.

I was embarrassed to talk in class, so teachers told my parents I didn't participate. My extroverted personality was dying inside. I became shy and rarely spoke to others. This is what it looks like when an insecure kid is dealing with a handicap. I had thoughts and ideas that I knew were worth sharing; I just didn't have the ability to speak them.

One day, after we'd moved to New Zealand, I was about seven and I came home in tears. I refused to tell my mum and dad what had happened. (They actually still don't know what happened to this day.) I was still the new kid in school and couldn't speak properly. Kids thought I was weird. During lunch, a group of boys pushed me up against the trunk of a tree and started kicking me in the stomach. They ran away when they saw a teacher walk outside.

~~~

My parents finally got me a speech therapist because I was so developmentally behind. Instead of coming every two weeks, which would have been the typical number of visits, my speech therapist came twice a week. She was a sweet, nonjudgmental lady who never shamed me for the way I spoke.

Another positive shift during this time was riding horses. Horses have always brought me a lot of comfort. The decision to have me ride was an intentional one for my parents because they knew I needed something of my own that gave me value and confidence. Horses have a unique gift to help people; it's why they are used in therapy treatment. Like many animals, they didn't require me to communicate properly and instead just read my body language. They also have the amazing ability to mirror our emotions, so on days when I felt sad, my horse would drop his head like he was sad too.

As the speech therapy began improving my articulation, my relationships at school started changing. Suddenly I had friends, and my sister no longer needed to be by my side. I felt a growing independence, and I loved making people feel good. Now all the love and warm feelings I had for others could finally be expressed! I've always had a heart for the lonely and the outcasts because I know what that feels like. Now I could communicate my empathy to them.

My parents told me and my sisters that our weakness can become our strength. People think I'm socially gifted, but it's really that I'm just good at reading people. I spent years not being able to communicate and sitting silently as my friends talked. I started spending time reading body language and studying people. I still do it to this day. People give away so much about themselves. I can meet a stranger and detect things about who they are because most of us walk around sending signals about our life experience. We are walking books, and if we take the time to stop and read others, we can learn so much without having to say a single word. So I learned how to read the books of people in the silence of my disability.

I remember thinking that my greatest weakness, my poor hearing, could become my greatest strength; slowly, after years of practice, I studied lipreading in earnest. It felt like the coolest superpower anyone could have because, to this day, I can be in a coffee shop and look across the room and know what people are saying despite not hearing their conversation.

I got better and cleverer at adapting to a life of partial deafness. Doctors have told me for years to use a hearing aid, and I've refused because I no longer see my impairment as a deficit. I don't tell people I struggle with deafness, and yet it impacts every single conversation I have.

~~~

My communication with the rest of the world may be foggy, but I've always felt that I hear God clearly. Have you ever felt like God is communicating directly to you? As if He has a message meant only for you? If you haven't heard God recently (or perhaps ever), ask the Lord to speak to you over this next week.

God speaks in many ways: through a verse that jumps out on the page, a loving thought in your head, a prophetic word, unexpected provision, a feeling of compassion during worship, warmth in your body as you pray, or a vision as you close your eyes. Each day is a treasure hunt where you search for the voice and presence of God. He is speaking to you; will you stop and listen? Will you lay down the expectations of how you think He should communicate with you and exchange that for wonder and open-mindedness? God comes disguised in everyday life.

My parents instilled in me the belief that I could hear God's voice just as clearly, if not more so, than any human voice. But just saying it doesn't make it so. I had to believe it. Hearing from the Lord is an enormous gift. You hear about people having "blind faith," but I had something like "deaf trust." Not everyone can hear Him, and sometimes you may go through a period of time when He seems silent. But during these times, I remind myself that I too am silent sometimes when around someone I'm comfortable with. It doesn't mean something is wrong between us.

Since I was a little girl, I've loved God because of who He is. He is the greatest, kindest, most loving, peaceful, and empathetic being I have ever met. So when I hear that voice, I know it's Him.

When I wake up in the morning, I pray this simple prayer: *God, please get to my brain before I do.* So when the world comes to praise us, shame us, reject us, or elevate us, we remain steadfast that we are the beloved. God whispers to us,

"You are my beloved child. On you, my favor rests" (see 2 Pet. 1:17).

"I have loved you with an everlasting love" (Jer. 31:3).

"I have written your name on the palms of my hands for all of eternity" (see Isa. 49:16).

"I have molded you in the depths of the earth and knitted you in your mother's womb" (see Ps. 139:13–15).

God's words certainly sound so much more loving than my inner critic. When a thought in my mind sounds like love,

I believe it's from the One who is Love. You will live through the highs and lows as His beloved. And you will get to hear this loving voice speak to you for all of eternity.

In kids' church, I remember noticing that many Bible stories dealt with pain. Between the partial deafness and surviving a tsunami, my life had already been touched by pain. God knew the pain I felt during these years. I would read about how Moses was almost killed as a baby or how the woman bled for twelve years or how Jesus was whipped and see that we all deal with pain.

The amazing gift is that God is willing to meet us in our pain. God is near to the brokenhearted. We can invite Him to walk next to us so we don't suffer alone. Psalm 23 tells us about God's presence in the valleys. We experience a unique type of God's presence during these times. God loves being the hero in our darkness.

~

I want to jump ahead a bit and tell you another story related to my hearing impairment. After college I moved from New Zealand to Los Angeles to complete my master's degree. I was twenty-two and my parents expected me to financially support myself, so I needed a job.

We don't tip at restaurants in New Zealand, so when I learned how it was done here in the States, I thought tipping was the best idea ever because I'm friendly and love people. I got a job serving in LA at a busy, loud American diner that served steaks and tacos. The dining area blasted jazz and pop music, and the kitchen staff shouted at one another. All the noise made it difficult to work there, but I was making more money working a few shifts per week than I had at my full-time adult job in New Zealand.

One of the biggest struggles was being able to hear people's orders, not just because of the noise but because often people don't treat servers very well—some view them more like a robot who delivers your food than a person. When placing an order, the customer may not even look at the server. Or they're dealing with a rowdy child and just shout their order. But if they turned away, then I couldn't read their lips. For most of my life, I hadn't shared my deafness with others. I just figured out a way to make it work, but this was pushing up against my limits.

My situation was made even more stressful because the chef was a two-hundred-pound, loud Italian man who was ruthless. If we made a mistake, he would scream at us. It was honestly pretty toxic, and he gave no opportunity for discussion. He'd work on the line, pacing back and forth in front of his kitchen staff, shouting at his chefs to cook faster, for servers to deliver food quicker. Everybody was terrified of him.

On one busy Saturday night, one of our regular customers came in. He ordered something but was talking to his wife at the same time and just kind of tossed it out there. I got the order wrong. I put in a $52 meal, but when I delivered it to the table, he gritted his teeth and informed me, "This isn't what I ordered." He made me aware that he was there all the time and that everybody knew his order. I picked up his plate and walked over to the chef and said, "I'm so sorry, he didn't want the filet; he actually asked for the prime rib."

The chef grabbed the plate and slammed it to the ground, creating a scene no one in the diner missed. I immediately sprinted to the bathroom and locked myself in a stall and cried. I only had a minute or so before I needed to get myself together and go back out there. I took a couple of deep breaths, wiped away the tears, and straightened my apron.

I slowly walked out of the bathroom back to where the chef was standing, convinced he was about to fire me. I'd watched him fire a server two weeks prior over a similar situation. He stood looking at me, shaking his head, clearly still fuming. I figured I had two options at that point: either say nothing or tell him why I got the order wrong.

Chef had his chest puffed out and he was scowling at me, towering over my five-foot-five self. "I'm so sorry," I said. "There's a reason why I didn't get the order right." I paused, feeling embarrassed and suddenly shy. "I'm partially deaf."

I watched as this big man, all puffed up, suddenly deflated. His whole demeanor softened. His shoulders dropped, his frown disappeared, and his expression resembled what I could only guess was empathy.

He immediately apologized for yelling at me and said he wished I'd told him sooner. I looked at him wide-eyed and my mouth dropped open; I was not expecting this response.

Right after this, I became one of his favorite servers. He started sneaking me food to take home after my shift, which meant so much as a poor student. He would send me home early to work on a research paper that was due soon. Then one day, I needed a ride home and he offered. While we were driving, I asked him why he had given me so much grace. He turned to me and said, "My daughter is deaf."

Wow.

Imagine if I had decided to let him fire me rather than telling him the truth. It takes a little more courage to put your disabilities on display, but look what can happen!

The two rivals of vulnerability are comfort and pride. Comfort would love us not to share the hard parts of our stories with others. Comfort chokes courage. Comfort is the public jail of the world, the Western golden calf, the antithesis of courage. We can never fulfill our calling and become courageous by staying comfortable.

Pride is another rival. Pride kept me from telling people I was partially deaf. Our pride keeps us from reaching out to others; it's much easier to isolate, to stick to the margins in classrooms, at parties, at lunchtime. The main reason we don't want to show people our weaknesses is because we feel those parts of us aren't lovable. The paradox is that when we share our weaknesses and make ourselves vulnerable, we're actually showing our strength. And we're modeling for someone else who feels isolated that it's okay to be weak.

During my time as a server, I booked a trip to go skydiving on a random Monday morning. What a wild way to kick-start the week, right? I was about to step out of the plane when I thought, *Riley, you have done a lot of ridiculous things in your life, and this is certainly one of them.* Then the instructor thrust us out of the plane (I was tandem skydiving), and we went falling down to earth. *Why did I do this?* But then I looked down and saw the beauty. I spotted the beach town I lived in and the coast with waves breaking on the shore. I knew it was one of the best decisions I'd ever made.

Then I thought about the times when I am about to make myself vulnerable (such as sharing my disability with someone or loving an enemy or standing up for myself). They feel just like the moment when I was standing at the edge of the plane, telling myself that I shouldn't do it. But then I do it anyway, and I'm so glad I do. Maybe it's your time to leap too.

6

The Gift behind Our Fear

"Fear tries to point a sword at your destiny."

When I was growing up, my family took birthdays to a whole new level. On the morning of my birthday, they would come into my bedroom singing "Happy Birthday," very much off-key, then cover me with kisses. The kitchen would be full of balloons and streamers, and we'd sit down for French toast, eggs, and bacon. Sitting at the table, I remember feeling so much joy. But then after the celebration, something took place that I dreaded every single year.

Mum would go around with a knife and pop all the balloons.

Something about the sight of her with a knife, popping those balloons, scared my little self so much. It started this irrational fear of the sound of popping balloons.

When I was eighteen years old, I went to one of my first-ever parties. Earlier in the day, I had spent hours swimming in the ocean, which after years of lifeguard duty was now my favorite place to be. The party was low-key, but tons of people were walking around the living room, chatting and playing games. I had a crush on a boy there. Truthfully, I'd had this crush for a couple of years, but I was just too nervous to talk to him. To say I wasn't confident around boys would be an understatement.

Finally, I mustered up the nerve to go say hi. I walked up to him and we started chatting when suddenly, I saw out of the corner of my eye that someone in the kitchen had grabbed a balloon and was holding a knife to it. With one swift poke, the balloon popped—and fear kicked in. Next thing I knew, I'd sprinted out of the house to my car, jumped in, and sped away.

Later that night, my crush texted me and asked, "What happened? Where did you go?" I was so embarrassed that I didn't respond.

The next year rolled around and I decided that enough was enough. I was going to face this fear head-on. I made a pact with myself that every time a friend had a birthday, I would go to the dollar store and purchase a bag of colorful balloons, blow them up, and give them as a little gift. The funny part is the balloons were pathetically tiny—they were maybe the size of my hand—because I was afraid they'd pop if I blew them up too much. It felt as if I was handing my friends a bouquet of drooping weeds instead of roses.

This balloon experience helped me realize that the more we expose ourselves to our fears, the less power they have over us. Constant exposure leads to tolerance, which can make us feel more confident to face those fears. You see, we all have fears. Maybe it's something small, like balloons or spiders, but sometimes it's something much more serious, like a fear of failure or rejection or getting hurt or losing control or dying.

Throughout my high school years, fear often took the driver's seat and made my decisions for me. When I was growing up, one of the things I felt the most passionate about was speaking to large groups. As a little girl, I'd come home from church and position each of my dolls on chairs and walk to the front and preach a sermon I had prepared on a napkin. One of my favorite sermons was titled "Are you a do-er or a but-er?" The idea was either you "do" for God, or you say, "But God, what about this?" I'd even added an altar call at the end, lifting the dolls' arms up to signify a 100 percent conversion rate.

I knew from a young age that preaching was my passion. I wondered, though, why the Lord would have me struggle to hear and speak. As the years passed, I continued to meet with my speech therapists to help me pronounce words more clearly.

One day in high school, we were taking turns reading a book aloud in English class. The teacher said, "Riley, it's your turn to read." I stood and looked down at the book I was holding, my hands shaking. I was about to speak, but then said nothing. I just stood there. Meanwhile, all the other students were looking at me. I was absolutely petrified of reading out loud because I feared my inarticulation would cause others to reject me. In the moment, I remember thinking, *Fear is winning this battle. . . . Fight back, Riley! Fight back!* But I couldn't.

After about two minutes, over the sounds of students laughing, my teacher told me to sit back down and asked another student to read. I walked out of that class so embarrassed that I'd let fear win. There I was, trying to do the thing

I felt most called to do in my life—to speak publicly—and I couldn't. Later that week, a girl came up to me and said, "Don't worry, I used to have a hard time speaking in class too," which was sweet of her to say.

The thing about fear is that it wants you to think you're alone. It wants you to believe you're the only one who deals with this problem. That no one else can relate. Yet fear is very much a shared experience. You may not be afraid to read out loud, but maybe you fear not feeling accepted by your friends or you fear going to a party because you have social anxiety. But once you gather the courage to do whatever it is you fear, you realize you are not alone. The thing you both love and fear is what you should pursue.

Like many other kids, I was scared of monsters under my bed. I'd brush my teeth and then sprint and leap onto my bed, tucking all my comforters over me. I'd feel so thankful that I'd missed the monster grabbing me by my legs. One night, I decided to lay eyes on this monster, so I turned on my bedside light and leaned over the edge. Nothing was there but a few old books. When we finally look fear in the eye, we realize it is so much smaller than we thought.

It reminds me of a time when my sisters and I were walking through the enchanted forest, the one on our farm. We had gotten lost in the woods and didn't have our dog Rosie to help us find our way back home. We were looking for anything that seemed familiar, but all the trees started to look the same. We got tired and hungry. Suddenly, we heard the grunt of an animal. Many animals, actually. Our area was known for having wild boars, though we'd never encountered any. Our parents warned us they could be super aggressive and might even chase a person down. They use their tusks like spikes to stab their prey. We couldn't see them, but it sounded like there were at least two dozen—and they sounded close.

My sister looked my way and said, her voice shaking, "How many boars do you think are in that pack?"

I decided the best way to respond was to underestimate the number. So I said very casually, "I think there's about twenty." A short time later, we finally put eyes on the creatures making so much noise. There, resting comfortably beneath a tree, were our vicious enemies: two little wild pigs stretched out in the mud.

My sisters and I didn't run away. In fact, we decided to get a closer look because we knew we could always climb a nearby tree. These two pigs looked grossly undernourished, all skeletal and puny. The reason I share this story with you is because our fears—the threats we believe are out to do us harm—are usually not as horrible as our imagination depicts them. In other words, fear wants us to believe the illusion instead of the reality.

When we think that fear is so much bigger and nastier than it is, we make rash decisions. I've heard it said that the word "fear" has two meanings: "Forget Everything and Run" or "Face Everything and Rise." It's important to note the two types of fear: hindering fear and helping fear. Hindering fear is the fear I had in class. It's the fear of being judged, of being rejected, of losing freedom, of failure. When we listen to hindering fear, we're not going to become our fullest selves. We're not going to live into the abundant life the Lord has called us to. I had a fear of commitment—and ended up friend-zoning the man who is now my husband because I freaked out. Had my hindering fears won, I wouldn't be currently married to my dream man.

Helping fear is the fear the Lord puts in us that acts like a bodyguard. It's there to protect us. It's the gut response or the subconscious clues or the survival instinct that comes when you have a bad feeling about something, like maybe you shouldn't walk down that dark alleyway or shouldn't go to that party. That's helping fear. This fear can help save us.

~

So now I have a question for you. The fear that you've been thinking about as you've been reading, is that fear here to help you or hinder you?

In my high school economics class, I learned about the concept of "opportunity cost." Opportunity cost is the value of the next best alternative when making a decision. It's what is given up between the best choice and the second-best choice. There's an opportunity cost to hindering fears.

Let's imagine you say no to an event because of your social anxiety. The opportunity cost may be going to that event and making a lifelong friend. Maybe you get shy and don't say anything to your crush. The opportunity cost may be going out on an amazing date.

You don't apply to a job because you're scared of failure, but the cost is advancing your career and landing your dream job. You freak out and don't show up to an audition, but the cost is being the main character in a successful play.

The opportunity cost of me not reading in front of my class was the ability to live a dream I felt called to—that is, to speak in front of people. I share this because when we choose to listen to fear instead of acting with courage, there's a cost. We will eventually get to a tipping point when we recognize that fear is taking too much control of our lives—it's costing us too much. We will have a catalyzing moment when we get desperate for change.

A week after I refused to read aloud in class, I was on my bed thinking about that moment, feeling embarrassed all over again. I realized the cost of fear. I decided right there that this fear was costing me too much. I wouldn't let my fear of speaking steal what I felt destined to do one day. I needed to overcome this fear. Maybe it's time for you to face your fear too. It's time to not let fear hold you back from your destiny any longer.

I decided to take my speech therapist seriously and practice as much or more than she'd asked me to. (Cue the *Rocky* music.) I practiced speaking in front of a mirror and at dinner. On weekends I'd sit my parents down and read a chapter to them. Fear was getting kicked out of the driver's seat.

The thing about fear is that it teaches you what you care about. You're scared because it matters. And you're brave because it matters. Think about those movies that have dragons in them. If there's a dragon, you know there's gold somewhere nearby. If you see and feel your fears, the dragon has appeared to protect the cave holding something precious. Behind the dragon of social anxiety is friends. Behind the dragon of depression is more joy. Behind the dragon of nerve-racking public speaking is something important you have to say. When you conquer the dragons of your life, you will find the long-awaited treasure. Slay the fears and acknowledge all the gifts you've been given. Realize your dream or adventure or relationship. Fear tries to point a sword at your destiny, but you can be someone who vows never to let fear make decisions for you.

The Lord does not want us to live our lives in fear. Jesus has so much empathy for what you fear and why. He walked this earth; He knows what it's like. He is the divine therapist, the miracle worker, and the most empathetic person. There's not an ounce of your pain that goes unnoticed by the King of the universe. He is aware of your every thought, your every emotion. He loves you so much right where you are, but He also loves you too much to leave you there. He wants you to move forward, past your fears and into a life of courage.

No fear is too big for Him; not those mornings when you can't get out of bed because of your depression, and not the nights you stay home because you feel scared. There is no feeling you've had that the Lord isn't aware of and hasn't felt Himself. He wants so much more for you. Don't let opportunity costs stack up.

When fear is in the driver's seat, it takes us places we don't want to go. Fear can push us into things we don't want to do. In high school, I was definitely the outcast because of my belief system. I felt so different from others my age. I'd never kissed a guy, I'd never been drunk or done drugs, I'd never snuck out of my family's house. Girls bullied me. They called me names. But I had heard stories about those same girls doing things to fit in. That wasn't me. As a result, I wasn't invited to a lot of parties because it isn't always so fun to bring the girl who won't drink and won't make the crowd feel comfortable about their decisions.

When I started high school, being left out made me feel really uncomfortable and awkward. But with each year that passed, I became less and less concerned with what people thought of me. I felt a strong desire to stay true to what I believed. I used to write questions to myself in a journal—for example, *Why is it that you don't want to get drunk?* Then I'd write out the answer. I prepared scripts for how I'd respond the next time someone asked me why I wouldn't drink alcohol or why I wasn't having sex. I started talking to my friends about it. I could feel my confidence growing. It was more important for me to stay true to what I believed than to let others shame me into a behavior that might hurt me. I didn't want fear to push me into a position that I wasn't comfortable with.

Another thing I started to do was write letters to my future self. I would write a letter to Riley for two years from now and express who I wanted her to have become. I wanted that Riley to feel even more confident and courageous and to not let fear push her around. I wanted her to still be committed to staying true to her belief system and to have stayed within the moral boundaries she set. I wanted her to be somebody I was proud of. I realized the Riley in two years that I'd be most proud of was the one who hadn't let fear guide her.

Every Wednesday night in high school, my sisters and I went to pony club. Our instructor told us that we had to fall off the horse one hundred times to be a good rider and taught us how to roll onto the ground and position our bodies so that there would be less chance of injury when we fell off. This idea started to rewire my mind. Yes, when I fell off, I was a little bit hurt and a little bit embarrassed. But my instructor was teaching me to not give up. If we keep getting back on, we'll come to the point where we get really good at falling.

We learn how to deal with fear and to not let fear stop us. Fear doesn't want you to make firm decisions; it wants you to spend your day in deliberation. Courage wants you to act and move forward. The whole goal of fear is to keep you from continuing in whatever it is you want to do. Fear wants you to never leave your house, to never leave your room. "Stay inside, stay comfortable," is what fear whispers in your ear. Comfort is fear's cousin.

Are there things you don't do because you're afraid? Is your goal to live comfortably? It's always easier to stay in your bedroom or in your comfort zone. But in your most honest moments, has your imagination gotten so out of control that it has begun lying to you about how cruel and painful life is outside of your comfort zone? I'll tell you what I was told: wipe the dust off your jeans and get back on the horse. Just keep going.

Eventually, your patience for fear's petty requests will run dry. Fear sounds like a bratty child. Go put fear in a time-out. Say, "No, fear, you are out of control. Go to the corner of my mind and sit in silence till I say you can speak." Put fear on the sidelines of your life. Fear won't go away entirely. It'll probably always have something to shout at you, but it's not running the show. It's not that talented. And after a while fear's requests become entirely predictable. Exposure will not guarantee fear's silence, but it will change your reaction to it.

To be clear, I'm not belittling your experience with fear. If our stories are anything alike, I am sure your fear is powerful. But I am belittling fear itself. Fear is weaker than your capacity to rise above it.

Your difficult situation might seem like too much to handle, but you've been here before. You haven't experienced the same thing, but you have felt overwhelmed. And remember what you did last time? You overcame. Dear friend, you have a lion within you who is ready to roar. It's time to rise up. The situation is big, but God is bigger. You don't need to know someone else's track record. Remember your own. You've conquered tough things before, and you'll do it again.

Life is not about living with no fear. It's what you do with your fear that matters. Ignore it, build it, face it, or master it. You choose. Cus D'Amato, a legendary boxing trainer, once said, "The hero and the coward both feel the same thing, but the hero uses his fear, projects it onto his opponent, while the coward runs. It's the same thing, fear, but it's what you do with it that matters."[1] It's your choice how you respond to fear: Will you forget everything and run or face everything and rise?

7

Saving a Life

*"Being courageous provides a greater capacity
to do more things that scare us."*

I have this life rule. It's something I try to hold myself to
every single day. It's so small, but it's changed everything
for me. Every day, I exercise three seconds of wild courage.
It's so small! 3-2-1.

Three seconds can radically change your life. Think about
all you can do with three seconds of courage. You can say
no, send the text, say "I'm sorry," kiss him . . .

I was twenty years old the first time I chose three seconds
of wild courage. But courage wasn't all that was at stake.
This time, someone's life was on the line.

I was living in Auckland, going to university for commer-
cial law. One weekend, I went to our family's beach house to
study for a huge test. I'm a super social person, so studying
while at school wasn't always productive. If I ever needed to

seriously study, I had to get completely off the grid and put myself in an adult time-out.

This particular weekend happened to be Valentine's Day. I was single, so the day felt like any other. Honestly, my heart was lonely for a sweetheart, but I enjoyed having time on my own. On Saturday morning, I woke up, ate some oatmeal, and after a couple of hours of studying, I decided to go for a walk on the beach. My brain ached from learning about insolvency and mediation.

Peeking out the window, I saw a storm had moved in. But I'd been stuck inside for too long, so I threw on a bikini under my black leggings and slipped a hoodie over my head. I grabbed my flippers in case I wanted to go for a longer swim. Despite the wild weather, there was no other place I would rather be. The ocean was my home.

I started walking down the pathway my parents had carved from the top of the hill where the beach house sat down to the beach. It's a bit of a dodgy pathway hacked out among the bushes and brambles, but I made it. Once my feet left the pathway and hit the sand, I took my shoes off. As I walked down the beach, I remember thinking how happy I felt to have the rain hitting my face. Not many people come to the beach in this kind of weather, and I saw no one else walking on the shore. I stripped down to my bikini and ran into the water, leaving my flippers on the shore. I wasn't concerned about the turbulent waves; by this point, I'd been lifeguarding for years and was a strong swimmer.

I dove into the water, plunging under massive waves. The water was pretty cold, and after swimming a few minutes, I thought, *Riley, what are you doing? This is dangerous.* Not only had the waves gotten higher, but I knew the danger of riptides. I started to panic, knowing it was not smart for me to be out in this. Luckily, I hadn't gone very far out, and I had been trained at spotting riptides. I swam to an area where the tide was calmer, but I could still feel the ocean trying to suck me out to deeper water. Meanwhile, my face was getting pummeled by white water.

When I finally got back to shore, I pulled on my clothes and sat on the sand, feeling like I should just hang out on the shore for a while. I was shivering, my hoodie pulled down low, just waiting; I was not really sure what for, but I wasn't ready to go back to my homework yet. In the distance, I heard the wind carrying what sounded like someone yelling. I pulled back the hoodie and scanned the shore. Near the shoreline, I spotted a man in waist-deep water frantically waving his arms. After years of training, that sight made my instincts kick in.

I leaped up, grabbed my flippers, and started running toward the man. Then I noticed he was actually pointing to something out in the ocean. As I studied the water, I spied a man about 200 meters (650 feet) from shore who'd been swept out by a riptide and was getting smashed by water. I started sprinting toward him, peeling off my clothes as I ran. When my feet hit the water, I instantly paused. I could feel the surge of fear rising up in me. What was I going to do? I didn't have my lifeguard equipment. I didn't have a radio to call for assistance. I was on my own. I could see that the guy out there was a bigger-sized man. I stood there, frozen, as my brain ran through the scenarios.

Then 3-2-1. I forced myself to run into the water.

The waves were smacking my face, and I was thinking, *I don't want to do this but I can't do nothing.* What were the odds that I, a lifeguard, a person trained to rescue drowning people in the ocean, happened to be at the beach at this exact time? I had to try. Standing in the water, I quickly slipped on my flippers, years of practice making the movement swift and familiar.

When I was 100 meters from him, I saw he was doing what in lifeguarding we call "climbing the ladder." When somebody starts to drown, they move their arms and legs as though they're literally climbing a ladder. He was spending more time with his head below the surface of the water than above. I had to get to him faster.

I doubled my effort and swam as fast as I possibly could, diving into the waves, entirely focused on the distance between us. I felt the adrenaline kick in and surge through me. I was in the zone. At that point, I wasn't even thinking about whether I'd made a good decision.

Finally, I reached him. I grabbed him by his shoulders and kept his head above the water. He was easily 250 pounds. I began shouting at him, asking if he could hear me, waiting for him to respond in some way. But when I put my hand on his neck, I didn't feel a pulse. I opened his mouth and it was full of water, and his body was stiff.

The man had drowned.

What was my next move? I counted to three again, and what I did next is still shocking to me. Somehow, my five-foot-five self lifted this unconscious man up on top of me, and kicking my legs as hard and fast as I could, I started slamming into his chest doing CPR from behind, using my body as a makeshift raft. I'd done this in training, but this was the first time I needed to get it right. I performed chest compressions, pumped his chest, and kicked my legs to keep us above water. Every pump was a desperate plea for his survival. I screamed at him to wake up, to come back.

When I reached the right number of compressions, I moved around to his face and blew air into his mouth. I started talking to God out loud. "Lord, I need Your strength." I remember thinking, *This is not over. This is not the end for this man.*

I continued pounding and minutes passed. I was losing energy. I kept praying. Then all of a sudden, he lurched and threw up but remained unconscious. I started shouting at him again but got no response. I put two fingers at his neck. It was faint, but I felt it—a pulse!

It's hard to describe how I felt at that moment. It was so life-giving, feeling that thump against my fingertips. I felt another wave of adrenaline rush through me, and I had the sudden belief that we could do it. This could happen. This man could survive.

I wrapped my arm around his shoulder and across his body to secure him while I began to swim, throwing all my strength into my one arm and my kicking legs.

The waves kept crashing against us, and on a quick check over my shoulder, I spotted a huge set of waves coming our way. The first wave hit, and I still held him firmly. We managed to stay together through the next two or three more waves, but the last wave was the biggest and hit us hard. The force of the wave tore him from my grasp. I lost contact with his body and watched as he started rolling around in the white water. Then he started to sink to the bottom of the ocean.

The same thought I'd had earlier popped into my mind: *This is not over.* I took a deep breath and dived down. I eventually pulled him to the surface and locked my arm around his shoulder before starting again to swim toward shore. It was a few minutes before we were close enough for me to touch bottom. As I neared the shore, his friend, the one who had been pointing earlier, came running toward us and into the shallow water and helped shoulder the weight as we dragged the man onto the sand.

I noticed the friend had a German accent. It turned out these two guys were German tourists visiting the Coromandel Peninsula on their travels. The peninsula has many beaches; it's not uncommon to have a beach all to yourself.

Up to this point, I'd done what I was trained to do—rescue someone from the ocean. But he was unconscious, and I was not trained to help with the recovery effort. In my head, I started begging the Lord to send help. This is when another crazy thing, a coincidence, happened.

Like I said, this was a small beach town on a stormy day on a random weekend, not a sunny summer day. At the same time the rescue was occurring, the town's local doctor just happened to be out for a walk on the shoreline, farther up from where I'd gone into the water. I hadn't noticed him.

He had watched as I ran to the shore and witnessed the entire event unfold, thinking to himself, *Dear God, there's gonna be two deaths today.* He wasn't a lifeguard. But he was trained to save a person once they'd been rescued. Not knowing what else to do, he called an ambulance when he saw me go in after the drowning man.

As I reflect on this experience, what amazes me is just how critical every minute is during an emergency situation. Even the timing of when the doctor called the ambulance could be the difference between life and death. There are no emergency services in any of the small towns in New Zealand, so one had to come from a city nearby.

Once the man was on shore, the doctor sprang into action and I stepped back. I remember the kindness in the old man's blue eyes. My adrenaline was slowly running off, and exhaustion hit me hard. A moment later I heard the ambulance sirens and watched EMTs run over. They asked what had happened, looking at me and this man who was twice my weight. "How did you do this?" one asked. All I could say was, "I don't know."

As they put the man into the back of the ambulance, he was alert enough to look at me and say, "Thank you." I later heard from the doctor that his recovery went well, but I never got his full name or contact information. The satisfaction of that moment was a testimony to me, deep down inside, that I had truly beaten my fear of the ocean. I'd seen the ocean kill thousands of people. What was once a place of death and destruction, a place that filled me with terror, was now the setting where I'd defeated the great enemy of courage—fear. I'd seen what the ocean could do. Now I knew what I could do, with God's help.

I pulled on my hoodie and grabbed my flippers and leggings. As I was walking back up the path to the beach house, I remembered how my dad had told me a decade earlier that all it took for me to overcome fear was to have a little more courage. I slowly made my way along the steep pathway to the house, feeling exhausted. When I got home, I took a warm shower, smiling each time I recalled what had just happened. Through this experience and many others like it, I was achieving my goal to use courage to beat fear.

~

When we use three seconds of courage, it might take us to our breaking point. I took MMA (mixed martial arts) training for years in my early twenties. My MMA coach would start the timer for my ten-round training at the point when I showed signs of being tired: sweat dripping down my forehead, heavy breathing, or maybe I'd asked for a break. He pushed me to be 1 percent better (faster, stronger, and more strategic) than the previous day and said, "Your breaking point is really your making point."

Your breaking point, according to Merriam-Webster, is "the point at which a person gives way under stress."[1] But the more stress your body, mind, or heart can handle, the further you can go. If an athlete can handle the stress of running faster, then the timer will show a new record. If a person can handle yet another breakup and not collapse in pain, then they can move forward with lessons learned and be hopeful about finding love again. If a CEO can handle the pressure and stress of meeting goals on a tight deadline, then they can make a greater profit. Success comes with the cost required to push past your breaking point.

Just as athletes try to push their physical breaking point, so we try to further our courage breaking points, the sacrifices and stress we are willing to bear to be courageous.

A few years ago, I went to a surf camp down in Costa Rica. The camp was in a remote location, and I had to take a tiny plane the size of a van to get there. It held maybe five people. Looking out the window of the plane, I saw small islands and cliffs. The ocean colors were a stunning blue and green.

The pilot didn't speak English, and at one point in the flight, the plane started shaking. A little boy sitting near me tugged on my shirt. I turned and he looked at me with his big green eyes and said, "I'm so scared." I smiled. "Hey, you know what? When I was a little girl, my parents taught me to put my hand on my chest when I felt scared. If I could feel my heart beating, then I was okay." The boy put his hand on his chest and looked at his dad. "I'm okay!" The dad looked over at me and mouthed the word "thanks."

The dad and I struck up a conversation, and somehow we got to the topic of courage. He told me that the previous summer, he'd decided that every day he was going to do something that terrified him. The thing that most terrified him was surfing because at that time he was fifty. "I'm a bit overweight. I thought maybe I'm too old or too unfit to try surfing." That year, he went from surfing white water that was a foot or two high to shredding down twelve-foot waves, which was why he was headed to the Costa Rican surf camp.

As he was talking, I thought about breaking points. When we're in situations that make us fearful, we can use three seconds of courage to push through the invisible wall in our hearts and extend the breaking point a little bit further. Being courageous provides a greater capacity to do more things that scare us.

Sometime later I had a professor at Fuller Seminary who shared an idea with his students; maybe you've heard it before. I want you to envision your tombstone. I know that sounds depressing, but try it just for a minute. Under your name and a line about what you were known for will be the years that you lived. The most important part of the tombstone is the dash between the dates, that little line that separates when you were born and when you died. What did you fill those years with? Did you live in a way that will lead people to remember you fondly after you're gone? My friend, I know you want to do something important with your life. You want your time on this earth to have a positive impact.

You want it to echo. Your life is too short to let fear write your story. Give courage the pen.

Three seconds of courage takes that dash and makes something out of it. It brings meaning to it. Just like the dad on the plane who chose to try something that terrified him, we won't learn how courageous we are until we push ourselves beyond what we thought we could handle and emerge on the other side braver than we thought we were.

Our courage isn't fully realized until it is tested. Every day, we have little tests that God sets up for us in which He gives us the opportunity to decide between courage and fear. For example, maybe you go into a coffee shop and your heart is pulled to that lady sitting in the corner. Maybe you feel like God wants you to go talk to her, to love on her. Or you get into a conflict with a friend, and have to decide, *How am I going to respond? Do I forgive them or hold a grudge?* Courage tests are all around us. Three seconds of courage is a simple tool, but it's what will help us grow into the person God wants us to be.

If someone who survived a tsunami can make friends with the ocean, every one of you reading or listening to this book is capable of wrestling with your fears until you've won. Doing deep soul work like this is painful. I know it's hard. The beautiful part of my story is that as I began doing the very things I feared, my courage grew a little more. Then at some point, something inside me shifted. I stopped thinking about myself and started thinking about others. Facing our fears is not only about us. On the other side of facing our fears is the gift of being able to help someone else.

Imagine if you could turn the very place you feared most into a place of victory and impact. The crazy thing about my life now is that I love to surf, and I love teaching others to surf. What if you could not only beat your fear but also teach others how to beat their fear?

In a world that says "you do you" or "stay in your lane" or "mind your own business," what if you lived your life differently? What if you chose to care? This is the ultimate type of courage because it will cost you something—maybe a bag of groceries, your precious time, or even your pride. But I can promise you this: living with the courage to care is the most fulfilling way to live your life.

Our little acts of courage are like little stones dropped into a pond. They send ripples out, and we don't see where they end. We don't need to.

When I think back on dragging that man out of the ocean, I'm amazed at how risky it was for me to be in that water. If I hadn't been trained in lifeguarding and had years of experience, I would never have run out into those waves. This brings me to one note of caution: we need to be smart in how we apply courage. Like the doctor who didn't run out to save the man, but instead called an ambulance, we must be aware of our capabilities. Have courage within the boundaries of your wisdom, training, and gifting.

Bravery without reason is like a compass without direction. Just because you're courageous doesn't mean you're applying your courage toward the right aim or in the right way. I enjoy jumping off rocks into the ocean, but before I jump, I check out where I'll land to make sure there are no rocks and the water is deep enough. Before you act in courage, assess the risk. Courage mixes well with common sense. So smarten up your courage and be brave with measured risk.

I want to also note that sometimes we aren't given an opportunity to use three seconds of *wild* courage each day. Occasionally, all we can manage is three seconds of *quiet* courage. When I was twenty-three, I experienced debilitating migraines that caused me to be bedridden in a dark room for twenty-four hours each week and in so much pain that sometimes I threw up. Quiet courage on days like this looked like texting a friend and asking for prayer or asking a coworker to cover my shift. Maybe for you, three seconds of quiet courage is getting out of bed in the morning to walk to the kitchen and say hi to your mum, showing up to a doctor's appointment, or booking another meeting with a counselor. Maybe quiet courage is simply enduring another day or seeking help when it feels overwhelming. For someone facing debilitating disease, mental illness, or any other life-altering situation, quiet courage might be the strength to take one small, hopeful step at a time, even when the path seems endless and shrouded in darkness. Your daily battles require immense strength and resilience. Though it may seem unseen or underappreciated, know that God is incredibly proud of your quiet courage.

You may not think of yourself as courageous, but it's not until you are put in a situation where courage—wild or quiet—is needed that you find out what you're really made of. A scientist will not know if his theory holds true until he tests it. You have to be tested by life and God and yourself to figure out if the theory in your head, the one that says you have courage, holds true. You may be pleasantly surprised or awkwardly shocked. You won't know until you push beyond what you thought you could handle and emerge on the other side. You may not have been successful, but success isn't determined by the outcome. The success is that you took that step in the first place.

So here's my challenge to you. Every day, do a quiet or wildly courageous act. Ready?

3-2-1!

8

Every Day Find the One

"Your true purpose is not found inside yourself
but beyond yourself."

A t twenty-one, my life on paper looked like a fairy tale. I
lived in New Zealand and had a great job working for
a charity that helps people become debt-free. I volunteered
at my church's youth group. On weekends, I rode horseback down the most beautiful beaches in the world and hung
out with tons of friends. But at times, I would catch myself
thinking about being elsewhere. I felt a nudge that life might
be more meaningful if I weren't so comfortable.

I believe we grow to the degree that we make ourselves
uncomfortable. So even though I was living a dream life, I
wasn't growing. The comfort zone is a beautiful place, but
nothing grows there. God is more interested in growing your
character than maintaining your comfort.

Think of it like this: the size of a goldfish is dictated by its environment. When placed in a small fishbowl, the limited space doesn't allow the fish to grow. But if placed in a more robust environment, perhaps a large pond, it grows much bigger. We are like goldfish. The environments in which we work, live, and play are the proverbial fishbowls that dictate our growth. The life I had created in New Zealand had become a small fishbowl, and I craved more room to grow.

I couldn't shake off the feeling that I was meant to be doing more. I journaled, asking myself why I felt so antsy in my happy life. I recalled a time after high school when I'd considered moving to America. I watched movies of college students in the United States and dreamed of being one of them. But when I left high school, I wasn't ready to take such a gigantic step away from home. I attended university in New Zealand and earned my undergraduate degree.

As a result of my restlessness, I started thinking about the people I wanted to be like one day, especially my favorite preachers. Where had they studied? Many of them had attended Fuller Seminary in Los Angeles, California. I started doing research into their Global Leadership program. The more I read about it, the more excited I got. I hadn't been ready to leave the nest at eighteen, and no one was going to push me out of it. But at twenty-one, I was ready to force myself out of the tree.

The Global Leadership program (Master of Arts in Global Leadership) at Fuller Seminary was an online degree. The seminary selected high-capacity leaders from around the world who had been active in their careers and further developed them as leaders using a multidisciplinary approach including missiology, theology, and psychology. Even though the master's program could be completed online, I started daydreaming about walking around the campus, getting acclimated with the culture of the seminary, meeting some of my professors, and attending electives in person.

I had enthusiasm and passion coming out of my ears, but I needed a target to focus on. This program would help me aim at my specific calling to use words, both written and spoken, to inspire others toward a more courageous life. The only problem was that the prerequisite for admittance into the program was five years (minimum) of full-time leadership experience in ministry. And since I hadn't become a full-time working leader when I was seventeen, I didn't qualify. (Although my sisters may say I got plenty of practice leading them at a very young age.)

I remained optimistic and applied anyway. I spent hours on the application, revising and polishing it until it was the best I could get it. Then I sent it in. One week later, I received a rejection email. The moment I read that email is etched in my memory; I was sitting on the edge of my bed, my eyes filling with tears, when I heard a quiet voice deep within me say, *And what will you do when I say yes, but man says no?* It was God's voice. I instantly thought of Proverbs 14:23, which says, "All hard work brings a profit, but mere talk leads only to poverty."

I decided to pray as if everything depended on God and work as if everything depended on me. When God says yes, we do our part to hustle hard for the kingdom.

Going after something you really want takes courage because there's a risk you won't get it. But if you feel so intimidated that you never take the risk, something of even greater cost stands to be lost: living your dream life. Would you rather miss out on your dreams, or miss a few shots along the way? As my grandma would say while tending to her garden, "Seeds not scattered never bloom." Likewise, dreams not tended never bloom.

Many of us stand waiting in front of a door. Do we think the door will open itself? We don't realize the door is motion-activated. It opens when we choose to step forward. Some dreams and opportunities will only reveal themselves when we move forward. Walk forth in faith. Make the move toward the people and the person you desire to become.

I didn't know for what purpose, but I knew moving to America and attending classes in person at Fuller Seminary was the uncomfortable thing the Lord was calling me to do. While I sat on my bed, rereading that rejection letter, something shifted inside me. Those welled-up tears never fell. Instead, I took a deep breath, pulled back my shoulders, and set to work on a plan to convince the admissions director to change his mind.

First, I responded to their email and told them global leadership shouldn't be defined by age or experience. Fuller Seminary should not only see who I am but who I can be. After all, the disciples Jesus chose ranged from ages eighteen to twenty-five and had little preaching experience. He knew how important investing in the next generation of leaders would be to His mission.

Next, I contacted some of my mentors in New Zealand and asked them to contact Fuller on my behalf, urging them to reconsider their rejection of my application. Then I drove to the biggest seminary in New Zealand, which was an hour and a half away, and met with the president to request he also email Fuller.

Last, I prayed. And I asked people around me to pray.

I didn't have five years of leadership experience, but I knew that oftentimes a person's determination informs their destiny.

I was in agony waiting for Fuller's response. Every day I thought about my rejection, but I remained hopeful that when I returned home, there would be a new message from them in my inbox. I just couldn't get over the feeling that I was meant to go there.

One night as I was talking to my parents about my heart to attend this program, I suddenly had the most brilliant idea. What if I moved to America now, even though I hadn't been accepted into the program, trusting entirely on faith that the Lord would provide? I have this rule in life: when making a decision, pick the one that requires the most courage. God gave me a gut instinct that it was the right move. The next day, I walked into work, quit my job, packed my bags, said goodbye to friends, and boarded a plane to America. Because my mum is an American, I too have an American passport.

I was acting like the miracle was already here, even though I had no evidence it would happen. Faith is obedience to God, and obedience is God's love language. Growing up, I loved the movie *Indiana Jones and the Last Crusade*. In one scene, Indiana must cross an invisible bridge to get to the Holy Grail. The bridge will only appear, however, when he takes the first step onto it. From where he stands to where he needs to be is nothing but a crevasse that goes down thousands of feet. This is blind faith, stepping out into the void, praying you won't plunge to the depths. That's how I felt moving to America. Faith is not about complete clarity; that is something you may never find. Faith is about simple trust in God.

Friend, what does your faith look like? Do you feel God calling you to something? What would it look like to obey even when it doesn't make sense?

I lived in America for one week, spending the time exploring the beautiful state of Colorado. As I was sitting in the back seat of a car with two new friends and checking emails, there it was. I let out a yell of excitement. I had gotten an acceptance email from Fuller Seminary! The Lord had performed a miracle. I found out later that Fuller had conducted an emergency meeting with their department staff and professors to change the rules for this particular program so they could accept me.

I didn't spend too long basking in this major achievement. The program would begin in a few short weeks, and I'd been visiting family friends in Colorado but hadn't yet found a place to settle in California. I searched online and found a cute place, located only five minutes from the university in Pasadena, California. I put down a deposit, sight unseen.

Looking back, I'm lucky I wasn't scammed. Although I have to say, the photos made the place look much larger than it was. Imagine my surprise when I unlocked the door to find a 250-square-foot converted pool house. Sleeping on a Murphy bed (which folds up into the wall) took some getting used to, and if the bed was down, I could be sitting at the end of it either cooking in the small kitchen or brushing my teeth in the bathroom.

I also had to adjust to the practicalities of living in a foreign country. Landlords and employers asked for my social security number—I had never even heard of that. I also didn't know how to drive on the right side of the road. (In New Zealand, we drive on the left.) Twice in the first week of living in LA, I drove the wrong way down a one-way road.

Walking into an American supermarket overwhelmed me. I stood looking at the milk section for ten minutes. I didn't know it was even possible to have more than fifty different options of cereal. At my local grocery store in New Zealand, there are a few cereal options, maybe five at most. But in general, there is only one option of most things, which makes choosing simple. I experienced analysis paralysis, which is when you can't make a decision because there are so many options. I was feeling loopy from staring at all the fruit loops!

In my new place in a new country, I experienced loneliness for the first time. New Zealand runs on an open-door policy for friends and neighbors, allowing people to walk right into each other's houses and borrow milk or sugar or whatever. I was used to hanging out with my friends every day. In LA, when I signed up for mixed martial arts training, they asked me for my emergency contact and I put down my own name and number because I didn't know anyone else. I began to wonder if I'd made the right decision. Did God mean for me to be here? To make this work, I would need to build a whole new life on my own from scratch.

The next item on my list was to make money. Near my tiny home, a well-known restaurant hired me as a server. You remember the chef story, right?

One night I was driving home from a shift around midnight, and a storm blew in. Without warning, my car engine died. I pulled to the side of the road and sat, watching the rain pelt the front windshield. Then I got out of the car, tears joining the rain on my face, and tried to fix it. Mind you, I have no experience in engine repair. I had misplaced enthusiasm that I could actually do something to get my car started again. But it highlighted a level of loneliness I'll never forget.

Sitting on the side of the road in the rain was when I decided I would put myself out there and make friends. Instead of waiting for others to seek me out, I would seek out those who might be feeling lonely too.

I prayed that God wouldn't bring just any friends along but the right friends, the kinds of friends who would make me love Him more.

To the person who feels lonely, God sees you. He cares so much about friendship. Jesus spent more time with his twelve friends than working and doing ministry. I pray you find friends who see the image of God in you, even if a bit of dust covers you. Keep praying until you find them, and when you do, tell them often just how much you appreciate their presence in your life.

~~~

Two other incidents occurred that first week in Los Angeles. The day after my car died, I woke up and took a walk through a park near my home. A man living on the street struck up a conversation with me. He asked me how I was doing and sounded genuinely interested. It felt like my first real, human experience since moving to LA. Although he was a stranger, I told him I was lonely and feeling down. "Well," he said, "the cure to sadness is to help someone." You might be thinking he said that so I'd give him money or food, but that wasn't the case. He offered me his wisdom, and though I wish I could have helped him in some way, I didn't have any money or food myself. Between the two of us at that moment, I was the sad one.

For the rest of the day, I thought about what he'd said. I wanted to turn his advice into something practical. If the cure for sadness came by helping someone else, then every day I would commit to doing that. If there was any type of courage I wanted to grow in, it was the courage to love others well.

When I got home from my walk, I stuck a Post-it note on my front door that read: "Find the one." Each morning, I'd pray for God to guide me to the person who would be the one that day (and to make it really obvious!). I prayed to know how God wanted me to love them. When I drifted off to sleep at night, I prayed for the one I'd found that day.

I noticed that finding one person every day caused my sadness and loneliness to decrease. It wasn't me that got myself out of this slump; it was me having my eyes on someone else. Instead of looking within, I looked at others. Your true purpose is not found inside yourself but beyond yourself. To have a purpose is to know that you are not the end goal, that you serve something greater than yourself.

God is writing a story on earth. We get to play a part in this, to cocreate a courageous story with Him. Our story is not just about our happy little bubble of a life but about how God can work through us to achieve something great for humanity.

How do you measure your success at practicing courage? I'll tell you what I think. The measurement of success is the one. Think about the story Jesus told of leaving the ninety-nine sheep to find the one. If one is not enough for us, how will one hundred or one thousand or one hundred thousand be enough? Improving one person's life is the measure of success. Sometimes one can feel like a small and lonely number. But don't let this little number fool you. One is a lot more powerful than you think.

~

The Lord created each one of us to shine with the light of God. A random thought occurred to me one day. Our smartphones, by design, cannot operate both the flashlight and the camera at the same time. You cannot shine a light while also taking a selfie. I believe this is because we are not designed to be the light and get the glory. When I started aiming the camera at something other than myself, I saw other people and let the light of God shine through me onto them.

The second incident that occurred during my first week living in LA was when I walked into a supermarket and noticed a lady at the cash register with little kids running around her. She swiped her card to pay for her groceries, but her card was declined. She got out another card and swiped that one. It also was declined. As the line behind her grew longer, the woman grew more flustered. The guy behind her said, "Come on, hurry up." My heart broke for her.

I left my trolley (what Americans call a cart), which was still empty because I hadn't started shopping yet, and sprinted over to the woman. Before she could say anything, I swiped my card to pay for her food. A mix of gratitude and embarrassment showed on her face. She didn't seem to know how to acknowledge what I'd done. Her kids ran off and she, unsure of what to do or say, walked away with them.

Afterward, I returned my trolley and drove home. That transaction zeroed out my checking account, so I couldn't afford to purchase any groceries. When I got home, I looked in my fridge and saw milk and eggs. I would have to make that work until my next paycheck, which was in a week. In that moment, I remembered a sign we had hanging above the stove in my childhood home in New Zealand: "Imagine if you woke up tomorrow with only the things you thanked God for today." I dropped to my knees and thanked the Lord for the eggs and milk. After all, the fridge could have been totally empty. I kept thanking Him over and over.

In France, people have a phrase—petites actions—that means "little things add up." We take small steps to accomplish a big goal. Finding one person each day will add up. It will increase not only the number of people you impact but also the amount of courage inside you to take the leap and care for someone else, despite the risks. You will become a person who is truly others-focused, and those are the most courageous people.

What would it look like for you to find the one every day? Your acts don't need to be big. It may be as simple as smiling at someone. One time I told a lady she looked beautiful, and she started crying. She said no one had ever said that to her! What if your petites actions could result in a person hearing something encouraging about themselves for the first time? I believe every single person in this world should hear they're beautiful—because they are.

Grab some granola bars and water next time you head to your car so that while sitting at a stoplight, you can offer a snack to a person experiencing homelessness. When you plan ahead, you set yourself up to bless another. What if next time you're in line at a drive-through, you tell the person at the window you want to cover the meal or coffee of the car behind you?

Few qualities are so highly prized as courage, yet it is in short supply in most societies. We have unlimited opportunities each day to act with courage—to show a stranger we care for them and send the message that they are not alone or invisible.

Imagine being motivated to find your dream job not only to make a living and support yourself but also to help a sibling pay for tuition or a friend pay down a large medical bill. There's having courage for oneself and there's courage that makes a difference to someone else. We radically love others when we stop thinking only about our own needs.

More than anything, the world needs this radical form of loving right now. The biblical story of Esther shows the power of courage and the radical love of others. Mordecai told Esther, in so many words, "Maybe you married the king for such a time as this, so that you could help protect the Jewish people" (see Esther 4:14). The courage she needed wasn't just for herself and her safety but for her people as well. This kind of courage is for every time and for all time.

~~~

My first week in LA, I attended a church in Hollywood. I noticed a lady with brown hair and a bob haircut, and because I'd been praying that morning for the Lord to show me the one, I thought she was it. I thought the Lord wanted me to go and encourage her. I hesitated because all around me were Hollywood celebrities. I worried what people would think of me. I allowed the fear of man to prevent me from approaching her.

At the end of the service, she stood and left. I never spoke to her. At home that night, I drew a picture of her in my journal because I didn't want to forget her face. I don't know what would have happened if I'd spoken with her, but I'm convinced she was the one the Lord had selected that day. But instead, I overthought it and let the "what-ifs" win.

We all know that feeling of regret at a missed opportunity to care for someone in need. Can you remember having a similar experience? When you felt compelled to do something but you stopped yourself out of fear? Did you see a car

EVERY DAY FIND THE ONE

accident and just drive by? Or witness a kid in school getting picked on but you looked the other way? What happens when we let the pressure of the crowd determine our actions? Courage is not the absence of fear but the assessment that someone else's need is greater than the fear we feel.

There will be times when we aren't successful. Not everyone we try to care for will be open to receiving help. Not every time we try to love someone well will it go as planned. And sometimes our efforts will simply fail.

We must consider failure as an opportunity to gather knowledge about what does not work. The not-so-easy truth is that we learn more from failure than we do from success. We don't actually learn much from winning. The act of failing, however, is a time to grow in wisdom, even if all you get is a greater appreciation for the desire and enjoyment of winning.

When I pitched my first book about the science of courage to publishing houses, I received over thirty rejection letters, and not a single publisher wanted to meet me. I had been waking up at 5:30 a.m. five days a week to write that book. I felt like a failure, until, on a call with my dad, he pulled out a John Maxwell quote that hit home. "Riley, fail forward."[1]

So I printed out my rejection letters and pinned them on a bulletin board on the wall next to my desk with the heading "Evidence That I Tried."

A year later, I pitched another book about my life and courage. This time, things went great, and you are now reading that book.

To this day, when I experience failure, I tell myself, "This is good for the plot of my life story."

Dear friend, promise me you'll fail. Because if you're failing, you're trying. And trying is the exact place you need to be right now. You may miss some shots at courage, but at least you can rest knowing that fear no longer has you bound to the bleachers. Also, failure makes your future success so much sweeter. Without the blood, sweat, and tears, the victory would not feel as remarkable. Without the embarrassment and rejection, the acceptance that success often brings would not be as satisfying.

~~~

People are watching. Others notice our public actions. When I paid for the family's groceries, I don't know who saw it. When you make an attempt at caring for others, whether you succeed or fail, you won't know who the bystanders are or the impact your actions may have on them. Or maybe no one sees, but Jesus does. And He is the only one who truly matters.

Have courage and do kind things regardless of who sees or how others may respond when they hear about it. If a soccer player looks at the crowd instead of the ball, they won't score a goal. When you act courageously, focus on the person you're loving. Let God choose how others will be impacted.

In this sense, there's no such thing as a failed attempt at courage because courage is not about results; it's about movement. Courage is like baking soda, a powerful ingredient that will raise your life to the next level. A little courage goes a long way. Likewise, every time you take action in the presence of your fear, you dilute fear's power and amplify your own.

When I was growing up, my parents would give me and my sisters their credit card while sitting in a restaurant and tell us to choose a stranger's breakfast we wanted to pay for. But the goal was to make sure the stranger didn't know we paid. Jesus's applause is enough. If we look for the praise of others, we risk involving our egos. Don't allow your ego to taint the act of kindness. True kindness blooms in the garden of humility. Give God the glory in everything you do.

As incredible as it sounds, you might even get pushback from other individuals when you're trying to help someone. One late afternoon, I pulled into a gas station near my place. It dawned on me that I hadn't yet found the one that day. As I was filling up my car, I saw a woman at the opposite pump about to start doing the same. I thought, *What if I paid for her gas?* It felt like the right move, and my bank account wouldn't collapse under this act of generosity.

I walked into the station, pointed out the woman to the man behind the counter, and said, "Hey, I'd like to pay for her gas too."

He looked at me and said, "No, you're not allowed to do that. It's against our policy." Mmm, excuse me, what?! I decided to be more assertive so he knew I was serious. I made direct eye contact, slowed my words, and restated my intention.

"No." He glanced at the security camera behind him as if to say, "My boss is watching. Don't push this."

I could tell his back was against the wall and he didn't have the authority to sanction my request, so I walked back to my car, disappointed. Why would they want to prevent someone from being generous in this way?

This may seem overly dramatic, but I am the kind of person who stays committed to my mottos. I care about what I think of myself and want to keep promises I make to myself. I want to set standards and live by them, every day. The judge of my integrity is my mind because I know what my true motivations are.

I never found the one that day.

At least, that's what I thought.

One month later, I went back to the same gas station and the same employee happened to be on duty. He recognized me and started walking toward me. I saw him coming and thought, *Oh no, I'm that pushy girl with the weird ideas.* Then I thought, *What if he tells me his boss watched the camera footage and he got in trouble?*

While my back was turned to him, he shouted, "Hey, you're the girl that tried to pay for someone's gas. Sorry about that, dude. I've wanted to say something to you since then. You inspired me to do things like that. Good things for strangers, like you wanted to do. Thanks for the inspo."

Ah! I had found the one that day. It just wasn't who I thought it was.

~

Back to my first week in LA. When I began this mission of every day finding the one, I started making friends. My personality helped as, in general, I see every stranger as a potential friend. After that night in the storm when my car broke down, I was determined to put myself out there and meet more people. I also knew that if I was feeling lonely, probably others were feeling that way too.

One year after my car broke down, I had moved from the pool house to an apartment on campus at Fuller. I was so excited to have my friends over for a dinner party. I couldn't yet afford a table but that didn't matter. I invited all of them, none of whom knew one another.

At 6:00 p.m., in walked George, a man experiencing homelessness and one of my closest friends. George was carrying his flute because he never went anywhere without it. Behind him was Jalin, a pro-MMA fighter who was winking at my conservative friend Abby from seminary who happened to be a passionate pacifist. Then a lady I refer to as my Black mama walked into the kitchen. I'd met her one day in Bank of America, and she'd insisted on calling me every week to make sure I'd eaten enough. If I hadn't, she would drop off hearty casseroles or other yummy foods. Then Chris arrived, another friend who, earlier that night, had been to a 12-step program for heroin addicts. Then came a few other friends from seminary.

There we were, twenty of us, sitting on the floor, breaking bread and laughing together. Dinner was nothing fancy, but no one left hungry. It was one of the closest things I have ever experienced to a physical manifestation of heaven on earth. Not only were unexpected friendships begun—with me and then among themselves—but I realized that night I had been healed of my loneliness.

If you're reading this, it's safe to believe there are people who want to be your friend. The culminating effect of growing friendships is becoming rooted in your community. Your community may last years or only a season. The fastest way to grow a community is to find a church home, serve at a youth group, start a Taco Tuesday, or open your door to new friends and sit on the floor breaking bread.

Community cures loneliness.

9

The Courage to Come as You Are

*"Come as you are, not who you wish you were.
Let others see and love your imperfections."*

Within my first month of moving to Los Angeles, I decided to join a Bible study to keep meeting new people. I found a group that met at someone's home in Hollywood. Driving to the first meeting, I felt a bit nervous because I didn't know anyone.

About forty people had gathered and were chatting before we began. It was instantly evident that this group was made up of artists and actors by their bright, unique outfits and their big personalities. We all sat in a circle and went around introducing ourselves. When my turn came, I said, "Hi, my name is Riley. I'm from New Zealand. I moved here recently, and I start my master's program tomorrow."

As I shared, I noticed one of the guys across the room staring at me. He had tight curly hair, big round glasses, and a kind face.

After my turn, the person next to me began their introduction, but the guy across the room continued to glance at me every now and again. When the Bible study finished, he beelined through everybody and came up to me, put out his hand, and introduced himself again as Blake.

"I have a feeling there's more to the story about the master's program," he said, smiling at me. "What are you studying?"

I told him about the Global Leadership program. "Wow, I have a friend who got into that program. I know it's a big deal to get in. Congrats." He asked a lot of thoughtful questions, and I found him interesting. It felt so good to have a deep conversation with someone, the first I'd had since moving. I sensed in me a desire for his approval. As we talked, he maintained unbreakable eye contact. He kept throwing out these big words and I had no idea what they even meant, so I just nodded and acted like I agreed.

"As I mentioned," he said, "I have a friend who is in your master's program, but she's at least ten years older. Honestly, I'm so impressed by you. You seem so clever and driven and unique and very beautiful. I can see why Harvard accepted you."

Wait, what? Harvard? Should I correct him? A few seconds passed and it seemed too late, the moment was gone. Then I started freaking out. In that one microsecond, I'd made a decision that would impact me for years.

Was it really a lie? I reasoned. I'd just chosen not to say anything. Later I learned about lies of omission—when you

134

lie by not saying something. I'd made a major mistake. This baby white lie grew into a full-grown monster.

Blake got my number and told me he wanted to hang out. He is one of those people who has a million friends. He was a photographer and many of his friends were artists.

The friendship grew quickly. The following week he invited me to his house to meet some of his friends. Whenever we went to social gatherings, he would proudly introduce me as "Riley who goes to Harvard." I would smile as people looked at me with respect and curiosity, when all the while my guts were churning and my conscience was screaming, *You're a liar!*

Fast-forward two years of friendship. I couldn't handle it anymore. I could have easily come clean to him, but I didn't. I would get all pumped up and ready to confess, then stop myself. I kept justifying staying quiet by telling myself that it wasn't a big deal.

But the guilt, just like in Edgar Allan Poe's story "The Tell-Tale Heart," wouldn't leave me alone. My guilt grew and grew until I couldn't take it anymore. I'm ashamed to say, I stopped replying to his texts and phone calls. Eventually, I completely ghosted him. When I look back on this, I ask myself, *Why did you lie, Riley?* I lied because I feared the opinions of others.

I believe at the root of most of our fears is this question: What will others think of me? We will go to great lengths to avoid scrutiny. But doing so prevents us from realizing our destiny because fear paralyzes us and keeps us from stepping forward. Instead, we're stopped dead in our tracks.

Every day, I thought about coming clean to Blake. I knew I would eventually have to face it; I just didn't know when or how. Can you relate? Do you have anything you desire to come clean about? Is there some hidden secret you want to confess? Then you know how I felt.

I took a class called Pastoral Care and Addictions as one of my electives. Our assignment was to attend six sessions of a 12-step program. These programs help people recover from substance abuse and addiction. People meet and offer each other support in a group setting. My professor advised calling ahead to see if the group was open to visitors. The assignment was to sit and listen. We were not to participate in any way but just be part of this very unique community.

The 12-step program I attended was Alcoholics Anonymous, and they met on Wednesday evenings. At the first meeting, I parked my car as far away as I could so I would intentionally arrive ten minutes late. This way I could avoid talking to anyone beforehand. I didn't know what to expect and felt apprehensive. I knew the reputation of AA as a place where people confessed secrets and held themselves accountable for their actions. That was an area I was keen to avoid because of the mess I was in with Blake.

The meeting was held behind a three-story cottage used for sober living. Near the front door a guy stood shouting at someone only he could see. I figured he was fighting with demons.

The room where AA met looked like a large conference room. A coffeepot stood in the corner, and people sat in a large circle on orange plastic chairs. When I walked in, people were chatting and laughing. I was struck by the diversity of the members. I saw a middle-aged white businessman in a suit, a Latina grandma wearing a colorful dress, a twenty-something punk rock star couple, a large man covered in tattoos, an elegant lady with brown hair cut in a bob and wearing Chanel, and a shy Asian girl who looked to be about eighteen.

My first thought was, *Church should look like this.* Imagine if in church we sat in a circle and aired all our dirty laundry, and those around us poured love and encouragement over us.

Here sat courageous people who had failed and were in pain. I found them utterly beautiful. In a world where people are classified according to their success, bank accounts, and social standing, I saw the faces of those who had been brave enough to show up for help. They seemed eager to learn how not to fail again. I smiled at a few people and sat in the back, simply observing.

A guy around thirty years old with black hair stood up. "Today, we're talking about steps 8 and 9. Step 8 is to make a list of all the people we've harmed. In step 9, we make direct amends to them, if possible, except when doing so would injure them."

The lady wearing Chanel stood up and raised her hands. "A burden has been lifted!" Her eyes sparkled as she explained the depth of her addiction seven years earlier that had harmed somebody and how the guilt of it had been eating away at her. She'd written a letter to this person asking for forgiveness. I saw so much freedom in her, and I felt a twinge of jealousy. She'd found the freedom I craved.

That lady's courage was contagious. I couldn't put off my own reckoning any longer. Although the meeting continued, I leaped up and ran out of the room. I had something to do that couldn't wait.

As I walked to my car, I pulled out my phone and left a voice message for Blake. Right before I hit send, I saw my lie to him as a splinter. Something that had started off so small had grown infected and was contaminating my conscience. I'd begun looking at myself with less respect because days and months and years had passed without me finding the courage to confess the lie to him. The lie had spread to every person he'd ever introduced me to. It may be a cliché, but it really was like I had an angel and a devil sitting on my shoulders, each whispering what I should do. I could hear my voice shaking as I recorded the voice message. The moment I hit send, I felt relief.

On the other side of a hard decision is peace. Put differently, if a decision you're making costs you your peace, it's too expensive. As you've been reading my story, have you thought of a friend you need to ask for forgiveness? Or is there a secret you need to confess? Is there someone you've hesitated to apologize to because you're embarrassed?

When we make mistakes, we often hold the keys to our own freedom. Not only do we need to seek forgiveness from others but we also need to forgive ourselves. When we are unwilling to seek forgiveness, it only hurts us.

I read an article[1] recently that said unforgiveness (or refusing to forgive) is now classified as a disease because of how much it physically affects our body. Unforgiveness causes feelings of stress and anxiety to increase, even leading to increased blood pressure and strain on the immune system. Refusing to forgive makes people sick and keeps them sick, according to Dr. Steven Standiford, chief of surgery at the Cancer Treatment Centers of America. Unforgiveness festers like a wound that won't heal. The truth craves the light, but lies fester in the darkness. When we expose a lie, we drag it out of the shadows into the light of day where it loses all its power.

I hope you can learn from my mistake and refuse to trade authenticity for approval. Authenticity requires vulnerability, transparency, and integrity. Show people the real you, no matter how they respond. Let them get close enough so they truly know you. Integrity is when who you are *is* what you do. The word "integrity" means to be whole, unified, and not splintered.[2] So when you live with integrity, you are the same in every environment; you don't change who you are for others.

You might be curious about how Blake responded. Within a day, he sent a voice message back to say he 100 percent forgave me. "It is not even that big of a deal. I still want to be friends with you. I still want to hang out with you. And in fact, I feel closer to you because of the courage it took for you to tell me." I no longer had something holding me back from true friendship with him.

After I attended those first 12-step meetings and met the requirements for my class, I decided to keep showing up to the meetings. I felt like I had found a community I had been craving and wanting for so long. The next 12-step program I visited was for heroin addicts. They thought it was awesome that I'd come to hang out with them, even though I was a "heroin virgin" as they called me. I attended for six months. Part of why I was so attracted to this group was because I'd never been in a room with more courageous people in my entire life.

Each week they'd share horror stories, stories of abuse and trauma—generational trauma—and they'd lift their sleeves and show me their arms, covered in scars from needles. They weren't just showing me their scars, though. They were showing me their hearts.

One guy who showed up to a meeting had relapsed the night before. He screamed and raged at himself for being so stupid. Some people around the room were shaking because their bodies were desperate for the drug. Others were pale, and some clearly weren't eating enough, their bones sticking out of their bodies.

They shared stories of going to the hospital after a relapse, of being the drug dealer at their high school, of not remembering anything from the previous three days, of frantically chasing that first high and never feeling satisfied. The saddest part of their stories was how they turned to heroin as a coping mechanism because they didn't know how to respond to the pain in their lives.

Some of the people showed up every single week but said nothing. I remember one lady who didn't talk but would sit in the corner and laugh this maniacal laugh that was off-putting.

Humor played a big role in these meetings too. At times when someone shared a story that made them particularly vulnerable, someone would crack a joke, and laughter would break the tension. It was a way of showing the person kindness, to lighten the mood and communicate that they were accepted and understood. It made me think about scuba diving. The diver goes down deep but eventually returns to the surface.

Attendance at these 12-step meetings was their effort to reclaim personal power. They were acting on their own volition and not allowing life to just happen to them. They wanted to heal and be self-controlled. They committed to keep showing up until they overcame their addiction.

Heroin is one of the hardest addictions to quit, with a relapse rate of over 80 percent.[3] One girl showed up twice, and then we never saw her again. We later learned she'd died from an overdose.

No one was shocked or judged anyone else's actions, probably because the culture in a 12-step program holds that every person knows their sin. They are accountable for their actions. How could they judge someone else for doing what they themselves had done? When you're covered in mud and you meet someone else also covered in mud, you don't ask how they got so dirty. If anything, their common enemy made them show each other more empathy.

Though I wasn't an addict, over the following six months I shared some tough times I'd been through. My problems were minor league comparatively, but the members of the group never belittled me. They taught me that I didn't need to act like someone I wasn't to be loved. I could just come as I am, share things I never thought I would share, and still have people look at me and say, "You're awesome. You're loved. Keep coming."

There were never boxes of tissues in these 12-step meetings. One girl shared the story of her abuse by her father. She wept and wept—I'm talking snotty nose and puffy eyes. I leaned over to the girl sitting next to me and asked, "Why don't we give her a tissue?" The girl responded, "We don't keep tissues here." At the end of the night, I asked the leader of the group why there were no tissues. I'll never forget his response. "Because we don't want to make a person feel like they need to clean up their face and pull themselves together. Recovery is messy, and the person never needs to feel like they need to appear clean when they're here."

This level of honesty hit me at my core. As someone who acted painfully positive growing up, I found freedom in a culture that embraced telling the truth and encouraged everyone to "come as you are."

I've often wondered what drew me so powerfully to this group of wounded souls with whom it seemed I had almost nothing in common. It felt like something deep within me connected to something deep within them, though I didn't know the first thing about drugs or addiction. I believe the connection point related to the experience of pain. This was much more than a lie that I told a new friend.

My kinship to this group of strangers sprang not from status or success but from the transparency of our encounters with pain. We had lived through hard, deep things, and we were still working to overcome them. But we'd found the courage to show up—messy and flawed. By telling our stories, we were facing ourselves in the mirror and saying, "I love you too much to leave you here."

In heaven, we will be sitting at the banquet table with people who don't look like us. Heaven will have a diversity of believers—from every nation, language, tongue, and tribe—all worshiping Jesus. We won't fight over whose cultural expressions are best suited for God's work. Before the throne, our theology and practice will finally be wed together perfectly and eternally for God's glory.

It takes such humility to show up and share with a room of strangers that you relapsed. Or to share the mistakes you made that hurt the people you love. People fell on their knees and admitted what they did. "This is who I am," one man said. I was in awe of them, a group of people who wore no masks.

When I was growing up, it seemed most people wore masks, including me. I'd put on a joyful mask or a mask that made me appear all put together. But in a 12-step meeting, I saw nobody trying to be anything other than who they were. They understood that they'd hear good things about one another, and they'd hear the very worst things about one another. And yet, without fail, they'd show up the following week and look each other in the eye. The only other place this happens is in a hospital, where people are sick and suffering and no one is trying to hide it. Attending those 12-step meetings was an exercise in removing my own masks.

I wish church and Bible studies could be like this. I wish we could all walk in and take off our masks. Instead, we often come to Jesus with our masks on, and He waits patiently for us to remove them. Masks aren't required with the Lord because He doesn't need our perfection. He wants our presence. He doesn't need us to have our lives all figured out. He wants the opposite! He wants to be the One who helps us figure out our lives. There is no experience or thought or emotion we go through that the Lord doesn't know. And yet, we tell Him, "I'm good." What if church was the place where we could hear Him say to us, "No, you're not. This is a place where you can come to me as you are and cry with no tissues available."

The heroin addicts' class was the kick start for me to do my own mental health work. I enrolled in six months of weekly therapy. I had to face that I couldn't remove other people's masks and acknowledge that I couldn't change them. But as my therapist taught me, I could imagine myself grabbing a piece of chalk, drawing a circle around me, and saying, "I am only responsible for myself, and it's time for me to take responsibility for who I am, how I act, and how I'm healing."

When I was younger, I could be an overthinker. I tried to take control of life, and it made me anxious at times. One time, my mum got a wet bar of soap and placed it in my hand. "Try to hold on to the soap really tightly." When I squeezed my hand, the soap flew to the ground. She gave me the soap again and said, "Now hold it gently with just a little bit of firmness." When I did, it stayed in my hand. "This is what life is like, Riley. It needs to be held, but lightly."

My therapy sessions were a time to relax my need to control and instead heal and grow. And I'm not done—I am a work in progress. The Lord reminds me to stay in my circle and take responsibility for myself because He has so much planned for me.

The first time I met Lisa, my spiritual mentor, she was the chaplain at Fuller Seminary. Students could book one-hour spiritual mentorship meetings with her. Although I no longer study at Fuller, for the past six years she has continued to meet with me once a month. Lisa is a stunning Black woman with keen, brown eyes. When you look at her, you see the Holy Spirit. At our first meeting, we sat down and she said, "So tell me your story." I told her about the tsunami and how I do a million different things to help others. She attentively listened and then she took my hand and said, "You could never do another good thing again, and the Lord would still love you." I burst into tears. That's when I realized I didn't need to strive and work to earn God's love. He loves me just as I am. This is what those people in the 12-step program discovered. They were worth getting clean and healing. I needed to learn the same lesson. No matter how messy and broken I am, the Lord loves me. He doesn't need capable; He just needs willing.

During this time of healing, I started to pay more attention to how I spoke to myself. I've said things to myself that I would never say to a friend, hurtful things, especially about my body. I've never considered my body good enough. One day during prayer, I had a vision of an old man and a young man sitting on a bench in a museum. They were strangers, both looking at the same piece of art. The old man asked the young man, "What do you think of this painting?" The young man started to rip into it, saying critical things about the colors and the style. The old man sighed. "Well, I'm sorry to hear you don't like my art."

When we downgrade or discredit the art, we do the same to the artist. The same applies to the One who made us. When we belittle how we were made, we're belittling God because He created a masterpiece out of every single one of us. And He doesn't make mistakes. He's like the sculptor who etches away at the slab of stone. The Lord is still etching away at each of us. He is forming us into works of beauty.

The truth is, at some point we'll have to let go of the expectations we've carried around about who we were supposed to be so we can fully appreciate the beautiful person we're becoming. We'll have to look in the mirror without flinching. We'll have to meet ourselves where we are and humble ourselves before we can be free.

We project a false self of perfectionism when we aren't given the freedom to mess up. People close to me know how much I struggle with perfectionism and achievement sometimes. Somewhere along the way, I convinced myself that I am a "human doing" not a "human being" and that my value is found in my productivity and perfection rather than being valued simply as a beloved child of God.

As a beloved child of God, I have so much more freedom not to be perfect because, in the end, it's not about me. It's about God, and God already achieved perfection through His own life on earth. It helps to surround myself with people who don't require perfection from me.

In my family, there was a high expectation for achievement and reaching goals. So as a little girl, I decided that my parents wanted me perfect, which wasn't true. They had huge expectations for my life, and they still do, but it's because of the high value they have for the preciousness of life. They've always stressed the importance of making a positive impact for generations to come. I witnessed times when perfectionism and achievement were rewarded and failure was shamed. I hated feeling shame; I would do anything to avoid it, even if it meant bottling up my sadness or anger.

When I moved to America and was on my own, I had the freedom to be whoever I wanted to be. I was a nobody in America, and my identity was a clean slate. I met people who didn't expect perfection and who liked me messy. Those friendships were deeper because when I was imperfect, when I fell apart, when I messed up, they didn't hold it against me. Imperfection cleared a path for deep friendships.

Imperfection also carves out a path for a deeper relationship with God. When we see our own limitations, we acknowledge our need for a Savior. There's room for Him only when we reach the end of ourselves and say, *I have no more options, there's nothing else I can do*. It's our pride that makes us think we can do life alone. Rock bottom is a solid surface to stand on as Jesus reaches out His hand to help us rise.

Being our authentic selves can be a bit of a battle, which is one reason we put up a false self when we're asked for more than we're willing to give or when we're put in a situation where we might get hurt. The real Riley is sensitive and feels big emotions, but from a young age, I saw how folks wanted, even expected, me to be joyful. The mask of joy I wore became a protection mechanism and kept me from feeling my sadness.

Almost all of us have had experiences that robbed us of our childhoods. We only get one chance to be a kid. Someone stole parts of our innocence. Sometimes we were robbed of the freedom to express our emotions. So we stuffed them down to carry on with the business of the day. But we should all be given the space to fall apart when we need to.

I pray you find friends who love your mess, who choose to step closer when you feel unlovable, and who want to help you heal your wounds. Jesus could have healed his wounds from the cross, but He revealed His scars so that we might believe. Let us show others our scars, so they too might believe in Jesus's redeeming love.

We have to accept that perfection is a myth. For the sake of our own healing and happiness, we need to understand that radically accepting God's unconditional love for us is the way forward. We must commit to loving ourselves through every mistake and misstep. We can stop chasing approval and start working toward a deeper understanding of who we are.

When we do, we'll see that the mistakes we tried to avoid became some of the most important parts of our story. The mistakes showed us when it was time to pivot. The mistakes pushed us to imagine better ways of living, and they brought us face-to-face with the fullness of who we are. Those mistakes weren't just inevitable—they were necessary. Somebody, someday is going to need the part of our story we're afraid to tell.

God is not shaming you when you make mistakes. Shame and love can't coexist. He does not hold these things against you. And no one is too far gone! Whenever you mess up or do something you regret, bring it to God and then say to yourself, *God has never loved me more than in this moment.*

My friend, it's time to let go of the mask. When you do, you'll hear others say, "Wow, you aren't so different from me. I am not alone." Come as you are, not who you wish you were. Let others see and love your imperfections. I hope you find people who are not burdened but honored to walk with you through any darkness. Let them know how you want to be cared for. I remember one time walking into my suitemate's room and asking for a hug. I felt ridiculous asking, but that hug made my pain melt away. Have you ever googled how many hugs you need per day? A lot! Your need for love or affirmation is not selfish.

You can't heal what you don't reveal. Reveal the hidden part of your heart to a trusted person. Shame subsides when stories are shared in safe places. Admission is the first step toward freedom and healing. Save up some extra money, call a therapist, and show up session after session to answer tear-evoking questions. Therapy is courage in the flesh.

Find someone wise who inspires you to be better and ask them out for coffee. Make your future self proud of the little bit of courage you use today. There is no freedom without responsibility, and now is the time to take responsibility for who you are. Shorten the distance between who you are and who God desperately wants you to become.

And remember, some people don't actually want the best version of you; they want the version of you that best serves them. But your authenticity matters more than other people's comfort. Be courageous enough to come as you are.

10

The Ministry of Presence

*"Courage is spelled R-I-S-K. The best risk
any of us can take is loving someone."*

I fully expected to grow academically and intellectually in
my master's program. I could already feel it happening
after my first year. While professors taught their students
about politics, cross-cultural communication and management styles, and international business, what surprised me
was the emphasis they placed on students' character transformation and intimacy with the Lord.

We talked about the state of our hearts. We were asked
questions such as: What does your time with the Lord look
like? How often do you spend time with Jesus? Do you have
hidden sins you haven't confessed? Is your heart spiritually
healthy?

When our inner spirits are healthy, our outward selves inevi-
tably become healthier. I saw evidence of this in my growing

friend community. For my first birthday away from home, new friends threw me a surprise birthday party. My love language is thoughtfulness. Surrounded by smiling faces, a pink pony cake, and handwritten cards, I felt so seen by my growing American community. I was consistently spending an hour with Jesus every morning. I enjoyed practicing sabbath on Sundays and turned off my phone all day. I even saw my spiritual health in my dating life! My youth pastor in New Zealand told me, "Riley, you date your self-esteem." Each of the American men I had gone on dates with was kind, emotionally intelligent, and loved Jesus. I also met regularly with mentors who encouraged me and called me higher.

I learned about mentorship from my master's program. We see mentorship demonstrated in the Bible (Elijah mentored Elisha, Daniel mentored Nebuchadnezzar, Mordecai mentored Esther). All my professors emphasized how important and life-changing mentorship can be. I selected five mentors for different areas of my life who became like my personal "board of directors."

I went about choosing my mentors by asking myself, *Who is someone I want to be like?* Then I would boldly approach them and ask them out for coffee. I'd come with preprepared questions (usually written in notes on my phone) to see if I had chemistry with and respect for them during our time together. If I left our time together thinking, *Wow, I feel so inspired*, then I'd email them to ask if they'd be willing to invest in a leader of the next generation as a mentor because I wanted to lead like them. I made sure to meet them regularly (at least once a month) but also made sure I fit into their schedule, not the other way around. For example, if they lived thirty minutes from me, I drove to their area to make it convenient for them.

All this healthy growth inspired me to start pouring into others on a larger scale. My first speaking event in America took place at a house in a low-income neighborhood with women who'd been rescued from human trafficking. To extend my virtual outreach, I started a blog on healthy sexuality. The blog was titled *Journal of a 22-Year-Old Virgin*, and I shared honest and funny stories of what it was like to be a virgin in Los Angeles. Publishing my first blog was nerve-racking, but I was blown away by how many young women wrote to me about their struggles to choose to trust God's timing amid a sex-saturated world. Others were shocked to learn I'd never slept with anyone nor even done more than kiss a guy.

And, of course, I still had my restaurant gig. One particularly intense Friday night at the restaurant, I finished my shift and stripped off my apron, which still had pieces of food on it. I plodded to the underground garage where employees parked; other servers piled out after me. My brain felt fried from memorizing table orders. I couldn't wait to get home and collapse into bed. "Hey!" one of my coworkers called out. "Want to join us for a drink at the brewery down the road?" We could always count on free beers and drinks there. Usually in that situation, I would say yes, no matter how tired I was, because I just love hanging out with people. (I once took a personality test that said I was 99 percent extroverted.)

"Thanks for the invite, but I'm headed home this time," I heard myself say. The words that came out surprised me, but I figured my body was speaking for me. The streetlights flickered as I headed down the steps of the garage, and suddenly I had this urge to run—as if I had somewhere to be and fast!

I flung open the door of my baby-blue Beetle convertible and sped toward the parking booth, impatiently waiting for the lady to take my money so that the arm would lift and I could exit the garage. I actually ran a red light on the way back to my place in Pasadena, the feeling of urgency growing inside of me.

My route home included passing over three historic bridges, each designed with white stone arches and funky but quaint street lamps. The bridge design looks to be straight off the set of *The Lion, the Witch, and the Wardrobe*. I crossed the first bridge and then the second. While driving over the third one, which is right around the corner from my house, I noticed something that caused my heart to drop.

In the middle of the bridge, I spied a dark silhouette sitting on the edge, feet dangling over a sixty-foot drop. The moment I realized it was a young man, I knew why God had wanted me to hurry.

I drove past him, then skidded to the side of the road. I ran toward him, adrenaline rushing through my body. When I was ten feet from him, I said, "Hey, dude, are you okay?"

No response.

I saw him staring at the immense drop to the concrete below. This bridge is not over water. I stood there watching him and contemplating my next move. I remembered seeing a video a few years before by a man named Kevin Briggs who walked up and down the Golden Gate Bridge in San Francisco, keeping an eye out for people planning to jump.[1] He said the best response is to remind the person they are not alone.

What could I say to make this young man feel not alone? I was at a loss, and then it hit me. It was followed up immediately with the realization that what I was about to do would put me at my courage breaking point, and I was pretty sure I wouldn't be able to push past it. So this needed to work. I counted in my head: 3-2-1.

I approached him, getting as close as I could to the railing separating us. Then I climbed over the bridge railing and sat beside him. When I got a better view of his face, I saw he was about sixteen years old and Asian. He wore baggy shorts and a green shirt with the album cover of some band. He looked impossibly sad.

Even though I was sitting next to him, practically shoulder to shoulder, he still didn't acknowledge my presence. I asked again, "Hey, dude, are you okay?"

Still no answer.

"What's your name?"

"Mason." Then he looked up at me, seeming startled to see someone with him.

He started talking to me. "You shouldn't be here, you shouldn't be here." His aggravation grew, and he spoke more aggressively. "You need to leave. What are you doing here? Go! Leave!"

I looked at him, recognizing the terror on his face because I'd felt a similar terror in my life. "Mason, you are not alone." I wrapped my hand around his.

He had nervous energy coming off him in waves. He said, "I'm going to jump. I'm going to jump. My life isn't worth it."

"Mason, your life is worth keeping."

He looked at me, his eyes so sad. I began praying in my head because he was now gripping my hand; if he jumped and didn't let go, I would fall right along with him. I felt scared not only for his life but also for my own. As I prayed, I heard the Lord say, *Find his hope.*

I needed to find a reason for him to choose life over death. "Mason, don't you think your friends would want you to stay alive?"

"No one wants me to be alive. They call me a loser. I have no friends at school."

"What about your family?"

"My family hates me."

"What about your mom?"

He grunted. Then I asked him about his dad. The moment the words left my mouth, I regretted them. His eyes flashed with fear and guilt and pain, and his body jolted forward.

"I'm jumping," he said, and he grabbed my wrist so tightly he cut off the circulation, later leaving a bruise. He slid his body forward, now more off the bridge than on it.

I felt portions of my life flash before me, and then, for some unknown reason, Mason leaned back, sighed deeply, and started to weep.

"My dad beats me." He explained how his dad often kicked him in the stomach so that the bruises wouldn't be obvious and kids at school would never know. His mom knew what was happening but did nothing to stop it. His ex-girlfriend cheated on him with his now ex–best friend, and he was failing school and dealing with depression and anxiety. He wanted to kill himself because the pain felt like too much. As he spoke, the tears continued to run down his face.

Lord, where is his hope? On instinct, I looked at his hands. The one closest to me still gripped my wrist. But his other one was playing with something, twisting it around. Then I recognized it; he was holding a guitar pick.

"Mason, do you play music?"

He nodded.

"Don't you think people would want to hear your music? If you die tonight, no one will ever hear you play."

He continued to stare ahead, and then he looked down. We sat quietly while he contemplated my question. I waited patiently for him to respond.

I noticed his body language shift. His shoulders seemed to relax.

With his legs swinging back and forth, he said, "Yeah, I'm actually really good at playing music." He said that he played the piano and guitar, even wrote his own songs, and sang. I stayed quiet and listened.

"I do. I do think people would want to hear me play."

The vibe changed from the intensity of a life-and-death situation to the prospect of a future. Mason's hope was resting on a single guitar pick.

"Can we get off the bridge now, Mason?"

He moved away from the edge, and we both hoisted ourselves over the railing to the other side. We stood looking at each other, and then I grabbed him in a huge bear hug.

"I want to tell you something, Mason. There was never a moment when you were out of God's sight. God is close to the brokenhearted. He is so close to you right now and wants to be even closer." I told him there is no greater hope than Jesus. Then I asked him if he wanted to give his life to Jesus and welcome God into his heart.

He nodded so I led him in a prayer.

"When you look away from fear, you get to look at something else. Look at the Father," I told him.

I explained how courage is found in sacrifice. When someone sacrifices for us, like jumping in front of a shooter, they show us how much they love us. The Gospel of John tells us, "Greater love has no one than this: to lay down one's life for one's friends" (John 15:13). Well, Jesus did more than take a bullet for us; He took our punishment. He took our sin and pinned it on the cross. That's real love. I told Mason how wildly God loves him. That if he was the only person on earth, Jesus would still die for him. I watched this young man who'd been so sad and filled with despair transform in front of me. His eyes held a glimmer of hope. The difference was undeniable.

We exchanged numbers and parted ways—him to his house, which was within walking distance, and me to my car.

Suicide is a dark force in the world that takes one person every forty seconds.[2] Mason's story reminded me of the story of David and Goliath. One little stone killed a giant. For Mason, this tiny piece of plastic, a guitar pick, killed despair.

~~~

Later that night, I sat in bed with my journal, adrenaline surging through my body. It took me hours to wind down. I wrote the entire story of Mason and then wrote a letter to God, asking Him to take care of my new friend.

I've mentioned this before, but it's worth repeating. Courage is spelled R-I-S-K. The best risk any of us can take is loving someone. Loving people well takes courage. We can sacrifice and not be courageous. But we cannot be courageous and not sacrifice. Loving others always costs something— your time, your energy, your pride, your privacy, your heart. I'm reminded of 1 Corinthians 13:4: "Love is patient, love is kind. It does not envy, it does not boast" (for full text, see vv. 4–7). A challenge I've set for myself, and maybe you can too, is to replace the word "love" in these verses with my name. Then I ask myself, *Riley, are you patient? Riley, are you kind?* Or I word them as statements: *Riley does not envy and does not boast.* Then I ask myself, *Am I living up to this? Would those around me agree with this statement?* If we want to have these traits, we absolutely need courage. There's something about courageous words. They give us the power to not only change our lives but others' lives too.

Every single day we interact with various people. Each one is in their own fight, facing their own tsunami. Suicide might not be what they're fighting, but maybe it's depression or anxiety or fear or self-doubt. Your kind and empathetic words to someone in the middle of a dark cloud can feel like a row of candles guiding them out of the darkness. Sometimes the most courageous thing we can do is simply show up. Being there physically, even if it's out of our comfort zone, even when it's risky, shows the person they're not alone.

People often will come up to me after a speaking event and share their struggles. I don't tell them how to fix their lives. Instead, I just listen. I'm not an expert or a therapist—but simply being physically present with them offers what I call the ministry of presence.

It wasn't my words that helped Mason as much as having the courage to simply sit down beside him on the bridge. Maybe you aren't ready to do that, but you can sit on a bench or a kitchen chair or a barstool. Don't be afraid to sit with someone in their pain. Don't be afraid to show up during someone's heartbreak or struggle or challenge. Sit with them in the silence; join them on the bathroom floor.

In the Bible, there's a character named Job. He went through the worst things imaginable. Every bad thing happened to him. He lost his work; he lost his family; he lost his health. When three friends hear about his hardships, they come to see him. They weep because they feel so much empathy for their friend. And then they do something remarkable.

They sit with Job for seven days and nights. Even more remarkable—they say absolutely nothing until Job finally speaks. God gave us two ears and one mouth for a reason.

Sometimes three seconds of courage means three seconds of silence. What would it look like for us to join our friends going through hard times and just be with them? It can be so easy to ignore someone else's problem. I get it. Our own lives already have too many burdens. The idea of sharing someone else's burden, being what Aaron was to Moses (see Exod. 4:14–16), when you're already tired and weak sounds like a lot. But in doing so, you get to remind somebody they aren't alone. You may be the only Jesus a stranger ever encounters. Your actions and your words represent God.

I know it takes courage and involves risk to join someone on their bridge, but you get to be the closest witness to somebody's progression from darkness into light. You get a front-row seat to what God is doing in someone's life. You get to watch as the Lord shows up and shows off in their world. Nobody else will experience that as closely and as intimately as you will when you choose to step into a person's life when they're going through something very hard. May you be the kind of person who "rejoice[s] with those who rejoice; mourn[s] with those who mourn" (Rom. 12:15). We're so good at the rejoicing part, at throwing confetti and celebrations, but not so great at the mourning part.

Psychologists have studied post-traumatic stress and how people respond after experiencing a traumatic event. Even when two people go through the exact same thing, they can have very different responses. Some people respond with post-traumatic growth, which explains the possibility of someone changing positively after a traumatic experience.

Studies show that people who responded with post-traumatic growth had one thing in common: a safe person who helped them process the trauma.[3]

The difference was a single soul who did not belittle or downgrade the person's experience but rather empathically listened and asked questions. A person who showed up even when the processing was emotionally heavy.

Imagine the look on Mason's face if I'd told him his life wasn't that bad and he was just being dramatic. You can be the difference between someone spiraling into a dark hole or that same person escaping cycles of pain and learning to grow in the light.

Psychologists have also discovered that people can grow through their pain by helping others. What are the tsunamis in your life? Could you take the hard-earned lessons from your suffering to help others in similar situations?

The original root of the word "courage" comes from the Latin word "cor," which means "heart." Brené Brown, a brilliant researcher, author, and public speaker on the issues of shame, courage, and vulnerability, translates the word "courage" as "wholeheartedness." "When it first came into the English language," she explained in her TED talk, "the original definition was to tell the story of who you are with your whole heart."[4] To tell your story with your whole heart; what a beautiful way to live!

Nurturing, compassionate, and caring people act from their hearts, and their actions produce courage. Loving your neighbors, befriending the lonely, caring for someone who is hard to love; all this happens because caring enough is really the foundation of courage.

But the courage to care can be messy. How far are you willing to go for love? Would you be willing to push that breaking point out even further? You can be the one who helps someone turn their stress into growth.

A few months after meeting Mason, I was sitting in a coffee shop with my spiritual mentor. She had asked me about the tsunami, and I was sharing the ripple effects of fear I continued to experience. I started to cry because I'd cycled through the same emotions so many times but *still* felt so much fear.

She looked at me and said, "One day, Riley, you will be in a room full of young people, some of whom are paralyzed by fear, and you will tell them it is possible to overcome their fear. Overcome it for that young girl who struggles to sleep, who is filled with anxiety. Do it so you can look her in the eye and tell her it's possible."

~

Now, reader, I have a few questions for you:

1. Who do you feel compassion for? Could God be moving you to help that specific group of people?
2. How can you show up with courage to help these people?

When you feel compassion for a group of people, that is often where the Lord wants you to serve—with your time and with your heart. God calls us to what we love and what we fear.

I'm compassionate for people experiencing fear because I know what that feels like. The very thing that broke me is the same thing I'm called to help others through. People who have similar wounds are the people we are called to help. They're still bleeding, and we know how to turn their wounds into scars. First, work on healing your wounds, then find others with the same wounds who could benefit from your support. Maybe you have a heart for young girls who suffer from social anxiety or for people struggling with body image. Whatever it may be, there's a group of people that the Lord has called you to love on. Go find them.

Because of Mason and because I survived the tsunami, I have traveled around speaking in schools about suicide. If someone commits suicide, that means fear won. In Orange County, California, during COVID, one school lost four people to suicide in one calendar year. I had the honor of speaking to the student body. Thanks to the tsunami, I know what the fight to choose life looks like. What emotion do you know intimately? We can empower people who are experiencing that same emotion to find the strength within themselves to change their lives.

~

I went through six months of weekly therapy, and after every session, a friend of mine would show up at my house with chocolate. We'd go inside, and sometimes I needed to cry and other times to laugh. She never tried to get me to talk about what happened in the session unless I brought it up. She didn't offer advice or tell me what I should do. She was simply there for me, nodding or putting her hand on my shoulder.

Over those six months, I ate so much chocolate! But I also felt my heart healing, not just because of the therapy but because of this friend who chose to show up and love on me over and over again.

I struggle with the lie that I'm bothering people or burdening them with my troubles. One day I expressed that to her. She looked at me and said, "Riley, your vulnerability is so precious to me. It is an honor to be here with you right now."

We can remind people that when they lead us into their storms, we consider it a gift and an honor. She would ask me this question: Do you need empathy or input? She showed sensitivity by asking if I only wanted to be listened to or wanted advice.

We only need one person in our corner. A single soul is enough for us to find the willpower to take the steps that lead away from comfort and into courage. Do you have a "show up through thick and thin" kind of person in your life?

Here's why I ask.

With billions of people on this earth, I know there's at least one person who would be honored to walk with you through the darkness of your pre-courage moment. There is a person who wants to see the pre-courageous you. The pre-healed, pre-successful, pre-blossomed you. And how cool it is that this person will then get to have a front-row view to your "courage moment" on the stage of life.

If you don't let people stand with you in your storms, then you prevent them from enjoying the beauty of your rainbows. If no one helped you carry your burdens, then no one will fully understand how hard you worked for your freedom, joy, and peace.

~

The ministry of presence isn't only horizontal (person to person), it's also vertical (person to God). We can guide ourselves and others to the Great Comforter. Remember how I told Mason he could look away from his fear and look at something else? The greatest thing any of us can look at is God Himself.

Close your eyes right now and imagine seeing Jesus, the most loving person you can possibly imagine. He is standing there looking at you with love in His eyes and His arms open wide, waiting for you to run to Him. He doesn't mind if you're running to Him to talk about the same subject over and over again, the same source of pain. He just wants you to run to Him; He's ready to listen to you.

It seems so small now, but once I was really stressed-out about finishing a paper for school. I called my friend and told her about it, and she stopped me. "Okay, Riley, you're complaining about it. But have you taken this to upper management?" Meaning, had I prayed about it? What a needless shame it is to carry burdens that should be told in prayer.

One of my favorite ways to pray is by writing letters to Jesus in my journal. The other day I opened my closet and noticed a box. Inside were all my journals, at least thirty of them. Those journals are full of prayer after prayer after prayer, written out to Jesus. I did that because Jesus is the best therapist. When you talk to Him without holding back, you discover that emotionally honest prayers bring peace, comfort, and strength. I give you permission to say brutally truthful words to a God who will not turn His face from you. He wants to know the matters and concerns written on your heart.

Consider pausing right now. Put down this book and write a letter to Jesus, telling Him everything you're feeling. (It's okay; I'll wait.)

Or write in your journal all the feelings you're struggling with, and then get down on your knees and pray for courage.

Pray for it over and over again until you feel the Spirit of God's courage within you.

One of the best resolutions I ever made was to have face time before phone time. When I wake up in the morning, before I look at my phone, I spend time with Jesus. I'm practicing the ministry of presence with Him and He with me. It's just the two of us. I do this every single morning because I know the Lord is the only one who can sustain me. Think of the line in the Lord's Prayer that says, "Give us today our daily bread" (Matt. 6:11). It's not weekly bread; it's daily. Our hearts need to be with the Lord every single day.

What if you set an alarm (or two or three!) to go off throughout the day to remind you to stop and pray? Pray for the person you're called to love. Pray for God to teach you how to love them better. Because if you want to love people well—if you want to live a life having the courage to care for others—then you have to go to the One who is Love.

I can promise you this, the more you choose to be with Jesus, the more you will become like Jesus. When I was five years old, I made this statement: "I'm serious about Jesus." And two decades later, I still feel this way. What would it look like for you to be a little more serious about Jesus?

Maybe you're reading or listening to me right now and you're thinking, *I don't even believe Jesus is real.* Try this. Sit down and pray for the Lord to show Himself to you over the next week. Then keep your eyes open for Him.

~~~

This book, the entire message of the courage to care, will fall short if you aren't praying. Prayer is the wind behind your sails. It gets you moving and keeps you moving. It is the source that sustains you. I can tell you this with certainty:

the satisfaction you've spent years trying to find through hundreds of different people, places, and things, you will find in one hour alone with Jesus.

There are always more things to do once you've prayed, but you cannot do more than pray until you've prayed. Prayers are like seeds planted in the earth. They take time to sprout into existence. Just because you don't see anything happening doesn't mean God isn't working. I dare you to pray so big and so often that when you get to heaven's gate, God will smile and say, "You kept me very busy, kid."

Your relationship with the Lord is the one thing that will give you the courage to love people well—to love them like it's their last day on earth. How would you change the way you loved if you lived like every day was *your* last day? Courage gives you the grit and guts to join people on the bridge. Courage sings songs of hope and sits with people in their pain, using life-giving words to talk them off the bridge.

You may be wondering what happened to Mason. Last I heard, he was leading worship at a youth group. He's made new friends and is using his hope to lead people back to the person who is hope: Jesus.

Courage can save lives. You can find other people's guitar picks. You can help someone find their hope. Your kindness will leave its mark on every heart it touches. An attempt at caring can go wrong, but I'd rather you live with "oh wells" than "what-ifs."

Be somebody who makes everybody feel like they're somebody. And remember, you will never look into the eyes of someone God does not love.

11

Make Your Courage Roar

*"Our courage earns compounding interest
because courage is contagious.
It goes on and on and on. Not until heaven
will we see the by-product of our sacrifices."*

My friend, people are waiting for your yes to courage.
One simple act of courage can leave a lasting impression on the people around you. Let me tell you when I first learned this truth.

When I was nine, my parents took our family to Thailand to volunteer at an orphanage that rescued children from human trafficking. This was the year before the tsunami. The orphanage was on the outskirts of the city of Chiang Mai. When we entered the building, which looked like a school, the space was filled with the sounds of dozens of children laughing and running around. They all seemed so joyful despite their circumstances.

We spent a week cleaning, playing with the kids, and doing whatever we could as a family to help. As a children's pastor, my mum spoke to several groups while my sisters and I made friends with girls our age. It stirred my heart to see that many of the children weren't wearing shoes. Blisters covered their feet and many limped because of the pain of walking on the rough pavement. Their playground was in the forest, making stepping on sharp sticks and rocks unavoidable.

When we returned home, I couldn't stop thinking about the friends I'd made in Thailand. Then I got an idea. Back at school, my sister and I went around asking students if they had any spare shoes they wanted to donate to the orphanage. (I knew they all had way more shoes than they needed.)

By the end of the year, we had collected hundreds of pairs of shoes. I couldn't wait to go back to Thailand to show the children what we'd brought them. We contacted the orphanage to find out how many children were there, and the number had gone up to one hundred. My sisters and I had gathered enough shoes so that each child could receive two pairs!

We flew back to Thailand a week before Christmas—a week before the tsunami hit. I was excited to meet up with the young girl I'd made friends with. When we showed the children the wrapped presents we'd brought, they were leaping around, laughing and jubilant. They started pulling off the wrapping paper and bows, eager to see what was inside. My heart broke a little because for some of them it was the first time they'd ever received a Christmas present.

Shoes! The children jumped up and began showing their shoes to one another. Then a girl named Anong stood up. She was clearly the leader among the older children. Everyone was bustling around, and Anong said to all the children, "Follow me."

We watched as all the kids left their shoes behind and followed her into a corner. She spoke in Thai so I couldn't understand her, but she was emphatic—shouting and waving her arms to make her point. One thing was clear, she was convincing them to do something.

Then the kids started nodding. The kids came back to the strewn wrapping paper and bows, and Anong approached me. She looked at me and said, "We will accept only one pair of shoes."

"What? Why?" I asked.

"Come and see."

The kids each put on one pair of shoes, grabbed the other pair, and started walking down the road. After about five minutes, we arrived at a Buddhist orphanage. Our group walked in and the kids clearly knew one another. Then each orphan gave the extra pair of shoes away. Oh, the looks on their faces! I was witnessing what it looked like to have the courage to care.

~

Anong taught me how contagious courage can be. The currency used in the Father's kingdom is love, and when we love, we serve. If you want to be wealthy in heaven, then love people and serve them well while you're here on earth.

I still think about Anong and the other children's actions. How remarkable that those young girls who'd endured so much at such a young age would choose to forego basic necessities to provide for their neighbors. Their shoes would wear out eventually, or their feet would grow too big. Instead of saving that extra pair for that occasion, they gave them away. Then again, isn't that what Jesus did?

As Christians, we strive to know Jesus and live like Him. That also means serving like Him. The more miracles He performed, the more people followed Him. But sometimes the courage to care, like Anong showed us, requires sacrifice, even of our basic necessities, like rest, so we can serve others.

I wonder, *What are you willing to sacrifice so you can serve?*

When I was younger, I loved helping out at kids' church. As I mentioned before, there were four services each Sunday. My mum got up at 4:00 a.m. to drive to the church because she was the family and children's pastor. I went with her so that I could help serve. I served at all four services.

People called me "the baby guru" because, for some reason, whenever a crying baby was put in my arms, they would stop crying. It wasn't unusual to see me walking around holding two little babies. Loving on children made me come alive. What better way to illustrate how we become our truest selves than by laying down our lives? When I'm serving others, I feel most alive.

I didn't care that I had to wake up early. It didn't matter that I had to be there for hours. I wanted to be there. Our courage earns compounding interest because courage is contagious. It goes on and on and on. Not until heaven will we see the by-product of our sacrifices. But that doesn't concern us because we aren't doing it so others will notice and praise our efforts.

Jesus healed the sick, cast out demons, and delivered people from their internal and external pain because He had compassion. Compassion means to be moved in the gut, for your heart to leap forward to a need. It means recognizing the suffering of others and taking action to help. The word "compassion" originated from the Latin "compati," which means "suffer with." Compassion is a tangible expression of courage for those who are suffering or in need.

You won't run out of people to feel compassion for. When I was growing up, my mum would say, "What breaks your heart makes your heart." The thing that saddens your heart may be the very cause God is calling you to help. Dear one, what breaks your heart? What moves you in your gut? Who would you be willing to forego your basic necessities to help? When you look at society, is there one cause or one group of people you wish you could help?

When I heard the stories of those children rescued from human trafficking, I knew that human trafficking would be a cause I wanted to help end. I not only collected shoes and went back; I also cried. Even though I was just nine years old, I started researching human trafficking to learn more about it while also thinking about what I could do to prevent young girls from being kidnapped.

Here are some clues to help you identify your passion. Have you heard about or seen an injustice that you can't stop thinking about? Did it make you curious enough to research it or ask questions? Did it move you to tears? A good way to measure whether it's a good cause to help is to imagine that if the issue got fixed or healed, would the world be a better place? Courage feeds our hearts. Fear starves them. There's a battleground in the eighteen inches between our head and our heart. Can we find the courage to enter that battleground and fight for people through our love and service?

In Mark 6, Jesus and His disciples went off to find a secluded place to rest, but crowds of people followed them.

173

Instead of taking a nap, Jesus preached. Later in the day, He knew the crowd had grown hungry. Scripture says that Jesus "had compassion on them" (v. 34); He was moved in His gut. He told His disciples to gather food so they could feed the crowd that had grown to more than five thousand. Jesus didn't serve out of obligation—He didn't choose to feed the crowd because He had to or because it would make Him look good. He served out of compassion.

The disciples brought two fish and five loaves of bread to Jesus, the amount one young boy had in his bag. I wonder, do you have some small thing you could offer the Lord? What's your secondhand shoe offering? The formula for serving is this: when we give God little, He makes it bigger. Jesus took those two fish and five loaves of bread and multiplied it so that everyone could eat their fill—and there were leftovers! God gives gratuitously; His love is abundant.

I believe the formula for serving is to give God what we can, even if it's not much, and He will multiply it to be abundantly more than is needed. It's the same with our courage. God can take our small efforts at courage and turn them into major feats.

~

As we approach the end of this book, I hope you've been thinking about what you can use your courage to accomplish. Maybe you want to start a business, show up to a social event you're anxious about, face a particular fear, or ask your crush out. But more important than achieving your dreams, I want you to not get lost along the way. I want you to remember that courage is not a vacuum of self-glory. Courage is practiced for the benefit of others.

In New Zealand, Six60 is a popular band of really chill guys my dad's age. In one of their songs, they say, "Don't forget your roots, my friend, don't forget your family."[1] I sometimes sing that song to myself as a reminder to never forget my "why." I don't want to forget that my courage to care for people is never about my own selfish ambitions. I do it because others are waiting for me to show them what is possible. Your people are counting on you.

Deep inside each of us, we yearn to make a mark on this earth with a stroke of courage that can't be erased. The most worthwhile mark we can leave is evidence of a life lived for others. When we live for others, not for ourselves, life is much sweeter and more fulfilling. Fear wants our potential to be trapped within ourselves. But courage taps us on the shoulder, points at our neighbor, and says, "Look, you are not alone, and you can make a difference in the lives of others."

What would it look like for you to be the conveyor of courage in the places and spaces you live—in your university hall, in your classroom, in your office, in your home? Are you known as a mover and a shaker? What are you going to do with the gifts you've been given to help people break free of the fear that binds them?

With each step of courage you take, a deep desire for success will rise in your neighbor's heart as well, whether it is your mother, a friend, or the person who follows you on social media. Regardless of whether they say anything, they notice the change in you. They hear you saying no, setting an earlier alarm, or talking about something new. That's one of the most powerful influences we can have: live a life that makes others question theirs.

When I was growing up, our neighbor had deer. If a fawn grows up in a field surrounded by a four-foot fence, it will never try to escape because it doesn't know it is capable of jumping higher than four feet—unless it sees another deer do it. The same is true for us. When we leap over obstacles in life, we open the minds of those around us. We teach others what is possible. When we believe we can accomplish something, we inspire others to do the same. My friend, be a fence jumper.

When the Lord called Moses to leave Egypt and take the Israelites to the promised land, the Lord didn't ask him to go alone. Traveling solo, he could have reached his destination much quicker. But God asked him to bring all the Hebrews with him. Have you ever thought about who your people are? Imagine wrapping your arms around them and saying, "I'm walking toward success, and I'm bringing you with me." Traveling alone makes for a depressing celebration party when you finally reach your goals. But if you travel with others, you're set up for a wild and fun party at the end.

When I was younger, I accidentally dropped an open bucket of white paint. Fortunately, I was in an old garage in a far corner of our farm; the paint splashed all over the walls. Our life is like that spilled bucket of paint. When we do powerful things, we leave traces behind that touch other people, not only now but in the future.

Ordinary people doing valiant things are changing and will continue to change the world we live in. You, my friend, are not here just to fill space or to be a background character in someone else's movie.

Consider it this way: nothing else would be the same if you didn't exist. Every place you've been and every person you've ever spoken to would be different without you. We are all connected. And we're all affected by the decisions of those around us.

My favorite toy when I was a toddler was an adorable little stuffed cow with big happy eyes that mooed when its stomach was squeezed. I carried Moo around with me wherever I went—dirt, sandpit, and all. I'd bite Moo when I was angry and aggressively hug and kiss Moo when I was happy. I'd use Moo to wipe my tears. Without my knowledge, my mum would replace Moo with a new Moo when the old one became too tattered by the ways of little Riley's wild life. I just thought Moo took a really good shower because, from my experience, my mum's showers were very thorough.

Even as adults, we sometimes need something tangible to hold on to—an object that symbolizes hope. Mum found out she had cancer when I was seventeen. She went through chemotherapy and her cancer hasn't returned. But the night she told us the diagnosis, we were all sitting in the dining room.

She said, "Girls, I want you to think of one thing you know God has called you to do." She waited in silence while we all thought. My sister Sierra wanted to cure cancer. Bronte wanted to go to the Olympics for horse riding. My dad wanted to give a million dollars to churches around the world. And I wanted to speak and write books that inspired millions of people to be courageous.

My mum held up a smooth stone. "Every time you see this stone, let it remind you to pray for your dream to come true." She handed me and my sisters each our own stone.

I kept that stone on my bedside table throughout college. As I grew older, I carried it with me all around the world. It was with me when I did my master's program. Whenever my hope was running low, I would hold the smooth rock and rub it, remembering how much I wanted to do this one thing for other people.

You may not have a rock, but consider finding something that you can use as your dream reminder. Whatever you choose, imagine it sitting and waiting for your courage to show up.

What is one nonnegotiable you demand from your life?

~

Every year my former landlord took turkeys to the park where people experiencing homelessness slept. On the third year, one of the men pulled her aside and said, "Hey, we really appreciate your turkeys. But you know we are homeless, right?"

She nodded.

"Well, maybe next time you can cook the turkeys."

I share this with you because our courage to help others requires planning. My parents would often say "planning precedes blessing." We have to prepare to meet the needs of others before the needs arrive.

Maybe after reading this book, you'll decide to do more random acts of kindness. You could purchase some ziplock bags and fill them with socks, a toothbrush, and toothpaste. Then next time you pull up to a stoplight or street corner and see a person experiencing homelessness, you could hand a bag to them.

Or what if the next time you walk into Starbucks, you tell the barista you want to pay for the next person's coffee?

Or what if you picked an orphan to sponsor who shares your birthday? Or dropped off a backpack with school supplies and a letter of encouragement to a local shelter or a center in a low-income area?

Or what if you bought chocolates and wrote sweet messages on Post-it notes and gave them to random people?

When we have the courage to care, we will encounter people who are not like us. Remember me sitting in a room of recovering heroin addicts? For you, this could mean reaching out to someone who is lonely or isolated. It could also mean standing up to someone who is being prejudicial or intolerant. Kindness goes a long way in changing a person's heart.

We'll also have times when the people we are called to serve aren't conveniently located in our daily sphere of activity.

Before Jesus fed the five thousand, He jumped in a boat and traveled half a day to visit a man who was demonized. The man lived in a cave and nobody would get close to him. Jesus arrived and they shared a conversation, and then Jesus healed him. Traveling so far to help one man may not have been the most efficient use of Jesus's time, but He sacrificed—both time and effort—for one person because even one person is worth it.

Are you willing to be inconvenienced to show someone love? How far does that love extend? One day, we hope to hear Jesus say, "Well done, good and faithful servant!" (Matt. 25:21), not "good and fruitful servant." We are responsible for our faithfulness, not our fruitfulness. When you adopt the lifestyle of having the courage to care for others, at times it may feel as though your efforts are not fruitful. But I want to encourage you to continue to be faithful. Besides, you will always have an audience of One.

We are responsible for loving people well; we aren't responsible for how they respond. Jesus cares so much more about obedience than results.

I visited South Africa with my best friend when I was seventeen. I'll admit, two young girls going to a foreign country alone is a bit risky. Our parents were hesitant to let us go, but eventually they agreed because my friend's family was from South Africa and we'd be staying with various family members.

My favorite part of the trip was going on safari. Sitting in a safari truck, we zigzagged through the game reserve. We had just seen rhinos and giraffes, and I was over-the-moon happy because I love animals. Out of nowhere, we heard a lion roar. I actually jumped in my seat because it sounded like the lion was nearby in the bushes.

But the tour guide assured us that the lion was two miles away. In fact, a lion is one of the loudest animals. Their roars can be heard from five miles away! We heard the lion but never saw it.

You can make your courage roar. When you live with the courage to care, people may not see you or ever meet you, but they will be impacted by your courageous actions.

God loves to respond to courage, like a father who leaps to his feet when his son scores a goal or a mother who claps when her toddler takes her first step. When we act in courage, we score a goal for heaven and the enemy tastes his inevitable end.

"Do not be afraid" is the most repeated command in the Bible. Having courage is the most powerful choice in any opportunity. But it requires effort. We won't just fall into having courage. A person of courage is who we become. It's the culmination of a thousand micromoments of grittiness and resilience, of determination to live a life that counts, though we may not see it for years. I didn't overcome my fear of the ocean overnight. We all love an overnight success story, but it rarely happens.

None of us are ever completely ready to take the risk or begin a climb we know is steep. It took twenty-five hundred years to build the Great Wall of China.[2] Talk about intimidating! But it was eventually completed, brick by brick. Courage is a decision to show up every day, to make sacrifices, to be committed. That's why it is so important to have your "why" at the forefront of your mind.

I have one last story to share with you. I was given the huge honor of speaking on the topic of courage for a TEDx event in Arizona. All the talks recorded from this location were posted on TED's YouTube channel for millions to watch. The TED organization is easily considered the biggest stage in the world.

I'd gone through months of interviewing just to land the spot. While in a store picking up my wedding bands, I happened to meet one of my heroes, Kevin Briggs, the man from the TED video who shared how he helped stop people from jumping off the Golden Gate Bridge. He ended up mentoring me through the process. Kevin helped me craft my speech. I scrutinized every sentence. Since I wouldn't be using a teleprompter, I memorized the fourteen-minute talk word for word. When I heard them introduce me, I walked onto the stage, stopping on the red dot as they'd instructed.

I looked out at the sea of eyes on me, took a deep breath, and focused on taking in the moment. When I was sixteen, I'd written that one of my biggest dreams was to one day give a TED talk. The producers gave me the cue to begin. I got four sentences into my talk, and my mind went blank.

Instantly my thoughts began to race, and I could feel sweat trickle down my back. I was frozen in front of thousands of people. I had a microsecond to decide what to do before panic set in and fear gained victory. Awkward silence filled the room. *God, I need You. God, I need You.* Then a thought bubbled up from the chaos and confusion. *Why am I here?*

Reader, do you remember what my spiritual mentor told me after I'd shared my feelings about the tsunami and how frustrated I felt to still feel so much fear? "One day, Riley, you will be in a room full of young people, and you will tell them it is possible to overcome their fear."

There I was in a room full of mostly university students who needed to be reminded that they could beat their fear. I thought of those who might be feeling alone in their fear, like nobody understood them. Just then, the words of my talk started coming back to me. I took a deep breath. "Everybody, thank you for your patience. I'm going to restart my talk." I heard a few awkward claps in the room.

I looked over and saw Jack, my husband, who was giving me a reassuring smile and nodding, holding a printout of my talk. Next to him I could see my parents who had flown in to support me.

I began again, and this time I remembered every word. When I finished, I heard applause rippling across the room. When I walked off the stage, I felt elated. I'd done it! A moment later, a young girl, a volunteer from the TEDx talk team, came rushing up to me. She was crying. "Thank you so much," she said. "Your talk meant so much to me. I don't feel so alone." And there it was. Every excruciating moment had been worth it.

~

Our lives are defined by opportunities—even the ones we miss.

The journey of a thousand miles begins with one step. We will never be quite ready. But we can choose to have courage, knowing the universe is waiting on us to be the difference-maker.

LETTER
TO THE READER

My dear friend,

I desperately want you to live a life of courage. I want you to be an old grandma or grandpa with wrinkly hands and a big smile, reflecting on a life of grand impact. Courage makes for great stories. You, right now, have the capacity to live a life and be a person that your past self would be impressed with and your future self would be proud of, full stop.

But this grand adventure with courage doesn't happen in a vacuum. You need people to cheer you along the way. You need what I call "courage cheerleaders."

My professor in my master's program asked if I would share my testimony in front of all the other students. It was the first time I shared my life story after moving from New Zealand to America. Standing in front of the classroom with all eyes staring at me, I was embarrassed to see the paper I held shaking.

I was about thirty seconds into my story when suddenly an Asian man named Albert in the back of the classroom who must have been in his seventies shouted out, "You've got this, kid." His words hit home. I straightened my shoulders and reminded myself that I did, indeed, have this!

Afterward, I went up to him and thanked him for his encouragement because it had been fuel to my confidence.

This became our thing.

Every time I sat down to take an exam, Albert would shout across the room, "You've got this, kid." An hour before a big assignment was due, he would email me saying, "You've got this, kid." When I told him I was going on the first date I'd had in years, a few minutes before my date was due to arrive, Albert emailed me saying, "You've got this, kid."

Albert even insisted on watching my first and only soccer game. I had recently met the captain of the soccer league team and thought he was cute. As a ploy to hang out with him more, I signed up to join the team.

Saturday rolled around, the sun was high in the sky, and it was game time. I spotted Albert sitting in the stadium in a puffer jacket and with a massive smile across his face. When he saw me, he shouted, "You've got this, kid."

I ran up to the huddle of people I recognized who were on the team. The captain introduced me to everybody else on the team, exclaiming he was excited to have me there. I blushed.

We warmed up, then it was time to play. The whistle blew and I was in position, ready to play soccer like a pro. For your information, I have no soccer experience. I had never played a proper soccer game in my life. I didn't know the rules but figured I'd learn them as we played.

People started running around, and the ball was moving so quickly that I couldn't keep up. I was running circles on the field, not sure where I was expected to be.

Fifteen minutes into the game, I hadn't touched the ball yet. But suddenly, the captain passed me the ball. Finally! I was so excited. I started dribbling and running as fast as I could toward the goal.

I was so fast nobody could keep up with me. In fact, it seemed like no one was even close to taking the ball from me. I heard people shouting and screaming. *They must be cheering me on*, I thought to myself.

I eyed the goal. I pulled my leg back and kicked it with all my strength.

I scored!

I turned around to look at the captain, hoping to see him smiling. But he was frowning.

Turned out I had kicked the ball into our goal. I was so embarrassed.

They substituted another player for me a few minutes later. I sat on the sidelines and wanted to hide for the rest of the game.

At the end of the game, the other team had beaten us by ten goals.

Albert ran up to me, gave me a massive hug, and whispered in my ear, "You've still got this, kid." I looked him in the eye, and he started laughing hysterically. Then I started laughing so hard I was crying.

Let's just say I had the shortest soccer career ever. The captain texted me the next day, uninviting me to any future games.

I cringe when I think of this story, but at the same time, I'm still proud of myself for getting on the field.

The thing about living a life of courage is that sometimes you'll feel like I did. You're going to feel like you completely messed up, and all you want to do is hide in a cave.

But will you enter the field? The choice is yours. Will you leave the comfort of the stadium and no longer be a bystander to other people's impressive lives? Will you step onto the grass and try?

Any attempt at courage is a lesson, not a failure.

I want to encourage you, my friend, that life is messy. You're going to get dirty. You're not going to get it perfect.

But you need to try.

Try and try and try and eventually, you'll get better. You'll even score a goal or two for heaven.

Be sure to find courage cheerleaders along the way. We need those people who, when we don't have the strength to rise up from the ground, will pull us up. Relying on others is not a weakness; it's a strength. Even more than this, it's the way God created us.

You only need one encouraging person to find the willpower to keep going. There are billions of people on earth, and I know there is at least one person out there who would be honored to cheer you on.

And I want to cheer you on too, so please tell me everything—your story, struggles, and dreams. I would love to be one of your courage cheerleaders. What's something you want to be more courageous in? What are you scared of? Send an email to me at rileywithcourage@gmail.com. I'll be holding a massive, colorful sign saying, "You've got this," as you run the race.

Love,

Riley Kehoe

NOTES

Chapter 1 Christmas in Thailand

1. "2004 Indian Ocean Earthquake and Tsunami: Facts and FAQs," World Vision, accessed January 19, 2024, https://www.worldvision.org/dis aster-relief-news-stories/2004-indian-ocean-earthquake-tsunami-facts.

Chapter 3 The Courage to Stay

1. Michael Casey, "Tsunami 10 Years Later: Is the World Better Prepared for Disaster?," CBS News, December 24, 2014, https://www.cbs news.com/news/tsunami-10-years-later-is-the-world-better-prepared-for -disaster/.

2. "Indian Ocean Tsunami, 2004," Australian Disaster Resilience Knowledge Hub, accessed June 28, 2024, https://knowledge.aidr.org.au /resources/tsunami-indian-ocean-boxing-day-tsunami-2004/.

3. "Ubuntu—I Am Because We Are," Olive Network, June 11, 2024, https://olivenetwork.org/Issue/ubuntu-i-am-because-we-are/24347.

4. Loretta Hieber Girardet, "Is the Region Safer 15 Years after the Boxing Day Tsunami?," *The Jakarta Post*, December 26, 2019, https:// www.thejakartapost.com/academia/2019/12/26/is-the-region-safer-15 -years-after-the-boxing-day-tsunami.html.

5. Mary Oliver, "The Summer Day," in *House of Light* (Boston, MA: Beacon Press, 1990), 60.

Chapter 4 The Battle between Fear and Courage

1. See Phil. 4:7.

2. Kara L. Kerr et al., "Parental Influences on Neural Mechanisms Underlying Emotion Regulation," *Trends in Neuroscience and Education* 16, (July 2019), https://www.ncbi.nlm.nih.gov/pmc/articles/PMC6756171/.

3. Imi Lo, "Invisible Wounds of the Sensitive, Empathic and Emotionally Intense Child," *Medium*, July 25, 2018, https://imilo.medium.com/invisible-wounds-of-the-sensitive-empathic-and-emotionally-intense-child-357a938660d2.

4. Vicky Yip, "Riley Name Meaning," Parents.com, June 11, 2024, https://www.parents.com/riley-name-meaning-origin-popularity-8630988.

Chapter 6 The Gift behind Our Fear

1. Wikipedia, s.v. "Cus D'Amato," last changed May 4, 2024, https://simple.wikipedia.org/wiki/Cus_D%27Amato.

Chapter 7 Saving a Life

1. *Merriam-Webster*, s.v. "breaking point," accessed May 17, 2024, https://www.merriam-webster.com/dictionary/breaking%20point.

Chapter 8 Every Day Find the One

1. John Maxwell, *Failing Forward: Turning Mistakes into Stepping Stones for Success*, reprint ed. (Nashville, TN: HarperCollins Leadership), 2007.

Chapter 9 The Courage to Come as You Are

1. Brenda Reiss, "How Does Forgiveness Affect Your Health?," Brenda Reiss Forgiveness Coaching, May 26, 2017, https://brendareisscoaching.com/2017/05/26/how-does-forgiveness-affect-your-health/.

2. Damian Cox, Marguerite La Caze, and Michael Levine, "Integrity," *Stanford Encyclopedia of Philosophy*, Stanford University, last modified July 26, 2021, https://plato.stanford.edu/Entries/integrity/.

3. "Understanding Why Heroin Addicts Relapse," The Recovery Village, last updated April 29, 2022, https://www.therecoveryvillage.com/heroin-addiction/understanding-heroin-addicts-relapse/.

Chapter 10 The Ministry of Presence

1. Kevin Briggs, "The Bridge between Suicide and Life|," YouTube video, 14:13, posted by TED, May 14, 2014, https://www.youtube.com/watch?v=7CIq4mtiamY&t=2s.

2. "Suicide Statistics," SAVE, accessed May 22, 2024, https://save.org/about-suicide/suicide-statistics/.

3. Xiafei Wang, Mo Yee Lee, and Nancy Yates, "From Past Trauma to Post-traumatic Growth: The Role of Self in Participants with Serious Mental Illnesses," *Social Work in Mental Health* 17, no. 2 (September

2018): 1–24, https://www.researchgate.net/publication/327613502_From _past_trauma_to_post-traumatic_growth_The_role_of_self_in_partici pants_with_serious_mental_illnesses.

4. Brené Brown, "The power of vulnerability," YouTube video, 20:49, posted by TED, January 3, 2011, https://www.youtube.com /watch?v=iCvmsMzlF7o.

Chapter 11 Make Your Courage Roar

1. Six60, "Don't Forget Your Roots," by James Fraser and Matiu Walters, Massive Entertainment, Ltd., 2011.

2. "When Was the Great Wall of China Built?," Travel China Guide, accessed May 6, 2024, https://www.travelchinaguide.com/china_great _wall/facts/when-built.htm.

RILEY KEHOE is a speaker, writer, and influencer. Born in London and raised in New Zealand, Riley has a master's degree in global leadership from Fuller Theological Seminary. A sought-after speaker, active blogger, and up-and-coming influencer, Riley has been featured on a TEDx Talk, interviewed by William Shatner for The History Channel, and published in several Christian outlets. She and her husband live in Franklin, Tennessee.

CONNECT WITH RILEY:

rileywithcourage@gmail.com

RileyWithCourage.com

@RileyWithCourage

@ALittleMoreCourage

https://podcasters.spotify.com/pod/show/a-little-more
-courage1

@ALittleMoreCourage

@RileyWithCourage

www.ingramcontent.com/pod-product-compliance
Lightning Source LLC
Chambersburg PA
CBHW030250100426
42812CB00002B/387